D1244662

URBAN RENEWAL AND THE END OF BLACK CULTURE
IN CHARLOTTESVILLE, VIRGINIA

ALSO BY JAMES ROBERT SAUNDERS

Tightrope Walk:
Identity, Survival and the Corporate World
in African American Literature
(McFarland, 1997)

The Wayward Preacher in the
Literature of African American Women
(McFarland, 1995)

URBAN RENEWAL AND THE END OF BLACK CULTURE IN CHARLOTTESVILLE, VIRGINIA

An Oral History of Vinegar Hill

by
JAMES ROBERT SAUNDERS
RENAE NADINE SHACKELFORD

McFarland & Company, Inc., Publishers
Jefferson, North Carolina, and London

British Library Cataloguing-in-Publication data are available

Library of Congress Cataloguing-in-Publication Data

Saunders, James Robert, 1953–
    Urban renewal and the end of black culture in Charlottesville,
Virginia : an oral history of Vinegar Hill / by James Robert
Saunders, Renae Nadine Shackelford.
        p.   cm.
    Includes bibliographical references and index (p.   ).
    ISBN 0-7864-0527-9 (library binding : 55# alkaline paper) ∞
    1. Urban renewal — Virginia — Charlottesville.   2. Urban policy —
Virginia — Charlottesville.   3. Afro-Americans — Virginia —
Charlottesville — History.   4. Afro-Americans — Housing — Virginia —
Charlottesville.   5. Relocation (Housing) — Virginia —
Charlottesville.   6. Poor — Virginia — Charlottesville.   7. Vinegar
Hill (Charlottesville, Va.)   I. Shackelford, Renae Nadine.
II.   Title.
HT177.C47S27   1998
307.3'416'09755481 — dc21   98-8758
                                                              CIP

Manufactured in the United States of America

McFarland & Company, Inc., Publishers
  Box 611, Jefferson, North Carolina 28640

For our daughter, Monica Renae Saunders;
Raymond and Yvonne Shackelford;
and the former residents
of Vinegar Hill

ACKNOWLEDGMENTS

We are grateful to the Afro-American and African Studies Program at the University of Virginia for allowing us to offer two courses under its auspices. One of the courses was a general African American studies course that provided students with an overview of African American history. The other course, actually entitled "Charlottesville Oral History," enabled those same students to go out into the "field" and conduct interviews with the former residents of Vinegar Hill, the vast majority of whom were senior citizens.

Aldon Morris at Northwestern University; Walter Allen at the University of California at Los Angeles; and William Elwood, George Garrett, William Harris, and Charles Perdue, all at the University of Virginia, offered important advice.

In our effort to recreate the history of events surrounding urban renewal on Vinegar Hill, we spent the greater part of a year in the University of Virginia microfilms room, researching old issues of the *Daily Progress*, Charlottesville's predominant newspaper. That task was essential, but also quite useful were the newspaper clippings that Marjorie Saunders, Yvonne Shackelford, and Jerry Ward sent us from time to time.

Numerous other individuals and organizations have been especially helpful: Ruth Eggleton of the Charlottesville Retired Senior Volunteer Program; James Herndon, Ronald Higgins, and Alice Pool of the Charlottesville Department of Community Development; Gene Arrington, Douglas Valentine, and others on the staff at the Charlottesville Redevelopment and Housing Authority; Margaret O'Bryant of the Albemarle County Historical Society; and Tina Eshleman and Matt Gentry of the *Daily Progress*.

Funding from the Virginia Foundation for the Humanities, WINA radio station in Charlottesville, and the city of Charlottesville itself enabled us to purchase essential materials, particularly cassette tapes and tape recorders.

Many of the events surrounding urban renewal on Vinegar Hill are indeed quite controversial, so we anticipated that there would be points at which we would meet with resistance as we endeavored to uncover what really happened. We were somewhat surprised to discover that there was no resistance at all. City officials were forthcoming with vital information, even when that information raised questions about their previous actions.

Other local citizens urged us on at every turn. And many black former residents of Vinegar Hill felt free, for the first time, to "tell it like it is." So many were depending on us to render an objective appraisal, to in essence recreate in the following pages a community that though no longer in existence should never be forgotten.

CONTENTS

LIST OF ILLUSTRATIONS

INTRODUCTION

Pre–Civil War legends abound concerning how Vinegar Hill, a 20-acre segment of sloping land at the center of Charlottesville, Virginia, actually got its name. One legend is that it was named by a group of merchants and hotel owners who prospered there during the early part of the nineteenth century. According to that account, those businessmen were Irish immigrants who, in dedicating the area, named it after the spot where an agrarian revolt had occurred in their homeland.

A different tale claims that vinegar itself was involved in how Vinegar Hill received its name. People hauling wagon loads of items had a difficult time ascending the hill. It was not unusual at all for one or more of such items to fall from the horse-driven vehicles used in that era to transport goods and passengers. As legend would have it, on one of those occasions, a cask of vinegar fell off, broke open, and drenched a whole section of the hill, leaving a pungent odor for a considerable period of time.

Another story makes mention of a cider-vinegar distillery that once existed in the area, a distillery that regularly released powerful fumes. Still another tale asserts that "vinegar" was merely a code name for the liquor that would later be produced and sold by bootleggers who made the Hill their base of operation. Now no one is certain which of the legends is closest to the true story of how Vinegar Hill, the neighborhood that grew to become the center of culture for blacks in the town, got its name.

The issuing of the Emancipation Proclamation in 1863 caused a great influx of blacks from their rural environments into various cities and towns. As the migration continued, Vinegar Hill became a focal point for black residential and social life. With segregation still intact, black businesses evolved to satisfy a rising demand on the part of blacks for a varied assortment of goods and services. By the 1920s these black-owned businesses constituted "The Prime of Vinegar Hill," an era of black prosperity that neither hitherto nor henceforth has been achieved by the black citizens of Charlottesville.

In 1954 the United States Supreme Court issued its famous *Brown v. Board of Education* decision, holding that segregation in public schools violated black entitlement to equal protection under the Constitution. The Court — after analyzing data concerning quality of equipment and buildings, salaries of teachers, and curricula — concluded that school segregation deprived black children of equal educational opportunity. That holding was to form the foundation upon which integration would be built in American society, though for years after *Brown*, the struggle for equality continued. "Jim Crow" laws, which reflected the general attitude of southern whites toward blacks, slowly began to be appealed. Blacks organized protest marches and sit-ins to bring the reality of the *Brown* case to southern localities. As a country we witnessed the deaths of Martin Luther King, Jr., Malcolm X, and John and Robert Kennedy, all of whom gave their lives in the battle to eradicate America's system of racial hypocrisy. One hundred years after slavery had ended, and 95 years after the 15th Amendment to the Constitution allowed black Americans the right of suffrage, southern localities effected the means to deny black citizens the right to vote. Fifteen years after *Brown* had mandated that public facilities be integrated, blacks still confronted "colored only" and "white only" signs.

As was the case with other southern states, there were powerful opponents to the process of integration in Virginia. *Brown* stipulated that desegregation of public schools should occur with "all deliberate speed." It was assumed that government officials and responsible citizens would not tolerate violation of the Constitution. Yet in September 1958 Virginia governor Lindsay Almond ordered that the all-white James Lane High School and Charles Venable Elementary School, both in Charlottesville, be closed to prevent racial integration. This act marked the culmination of a statewide series of events aimed at stopping blacks from gaining access to public facilities designated "white." In fact, such action, also known as "massive resistance," delayed the execution of the *Brown* mandate for as long as a decade in some parts of Virginia.

But blacks in Charlottesville had a resistance plan of their own. Parents of black students who had been selected to integrate the Charlottesville white schools refused to return their children to all-black city schools. They arranged instead for the children to receive academic instruction at home through the assistance of special tutors and retired school teachers, or at the school board main office where several levels of education were taught in a single room. Meanwhile, white students, because their schools had been closed, attended private tutoring sessions at churches, in individual homes, and at other locations throughout the city. This stalemate finally ended in January 1959, when the pressure to integrate intensified. Under extreme pressure the white public schools finally reopened, and the process of integration resumed.

With this as an historic backdrop, a Charlottesville referendum was conducted on June 14, 1960. Voters were asked to determine whether it was necessary to redevelop the Vinegar Hill area. At the time, prospective voters were required to pay a $1.50 poll tax. Many buildings on the Hill were deteriorating, particularly the nineteenth-century frame houses and clapboard structures that still lingered in certain sections of the neighborhood. "A country-style slum" was how some regarded the area, and it was not unusual to see outdoor privies, outdoor water spigots, and grassless yards filled with abandoned toys and debris. Some residents raised farm animals, including pigs and chickens; others attempted to maintain fruit and vegetable gardens. So in essence, by the 1950s this 20-acre tract of land combined both rural and urban elements, all meshed together in the center of a developing city.

But as mentioned before, the Hill was by then also the center of black social life. It was the locale for organizations such as the Odd Fellows, the Masons, the Elks, and Eastern Star. For decades it was the site of the city's only black school. Black churches were on the Hill, and on Saturday evenings the Blue Diamond Nightclub hummed the strains of the latest jazz tunes.

In January 1954 the Charlottesville City Council had adopted a resolution stating that "unsanitary and unsafe inhabited dwelling accommodations exist in the city" and "there is a shortage of safe and sanitary dwelling accommodations in the city" and "such condition can best be overcome by the establishment of a Housing Authority." That same year a referendum was held on the question: "Is there a need for a Housing Authority to be activated in the City of Charlottesville?" The voters who favored having a housing authority numbered 1,105; those against it totaled 1,069. Subsequently, on June 23, 1954, the mayor appointed the authority's first members. Then after years of resolutions, recommendations, and special General Assembly charter amendments, the June 14, 1960, redevelopment referendum was passed by a very narrow margin.

Just prior to that latter referendum, newspaper advertisements offered lists of the advantages and disadvantages of urban renewal on the Hill. The advantages were presented as being much more profound, including higher property values, better stores, wider streets, new apartment buildings, elimination of slums, and federal assistance amounting to as much as two-thirds of the net project cost. The disadvantages listed were not so numerous. Only two negative prospects were elaborated upon at any length. One disadvantage of urban renewal as planned for the Hill was that the federal government could intervene in local policies related to the project. The other cause for apprehension was that redevelopment might have meant the shifting of slum conditions from one section of the city to another.

An issue not given nearly enough public consideration was the commercial value of the Hill. By the time the demolition part of urban renewal had been completed in 1965, 29 businesses had been disrupted. They consisted of black restaurants and grocery stores, as well as furniture stores, barbershops, antique shops, an insurance agency, a clothing store, a shoe repair shop, a drugstore, and a hat-cleaning establishment. The city of Charlottesville reported in a 1960 survey that the 29 businesses had a combined gross income of $1.6 million for the preceding year. Several of the smaller shops had been experiencing financial difficulty as a result of increased industrialization and the broadened competitive market. Yet they had continued their operations in what was, for most, the only section of town in which their businesses could have thrived. The proprietors of those businesses were paid fair market value for their buildings and also compensated for costs involved in moving stock and equipment.

Individual homeowners were also compensated fair market value for their buildings. Furthermore, they were paid an additional $5,000, as well as reasonable moving expenses. So dilapidated buildings were not the only structures destroyed. Well-maintained homes with indoor plumbing, gas heat, and other modern conveniences were demolished during the renewal project.

Of the 136 renters who resided on the Hill at the time of renewal, 119 were black. All of the renters were allowed compensation to aid them in moving to the public housing complex built as part of the renewal plan. That low-income housing development, built in a different section of town, was given the name "Westhaven" as a tribute to one of Charlottesville's early black entrepreneurs. Still, though the housing project may initially have been attractive to some of the tenants who were relocated from the Hill, the Westhaven housing project has since taken on characteristics typical of other such inner-city housing projects. Most tellingly, its overcrowded conditions represent a density nearly three times that of the rest of the city. One of the most feared potential disadvantages of urban renewal had come to fruition; one slum area indeed had been substituted for another.

Questions remain concerning what the ultimate effects of urban renewal have been. More than the two-thirds federal assistance originally projected, the whole Vinegar Hill project by the mid–1960s had actually involved the use of $2.4 million in federal funds and $608,000 in local tax monies, quite a bargain if you look at it from a local governmental perspective. But from a different point of view, urban renewal as it took place on the Hill has profoundly tragic implications.

As demolition crews worked to level this significant portion of the central city, 600 individuals were uprooted. Most were hesitant to move; they viewed the move with uncertainty and anticipation. Some were bitter over their sense of helplessness as the city exercised its prerogative of "eminent domain." Two elderly individuals died during the process of relocation, and several others succumbed soon after displacement. Now, one might say that these elderly people were destined to die soon anyway. How do we know that urban renewal was to blame? The fact of the matter is that we do not know for sure, but it is important to consider whether being uprooted from their homes caused some, especially the elderly who had been there for generations, enough psychological suffering that they no longer wished to live.

The then director of the Charlottesville Redevelopment and Housing Authority, Gene Arrington, maintained that many residents of Westhaven expressed appreciation for their improved living environment. For some, the move to the newly constructed project had meant first-time exposure to such conveniences as hot running water, indoor toilets, and electricity. However, since those initial years of the renewal project, Westhaven has become just another economically depressed and isolated black community. Teenage boys see no hope in the educational system. Teenage girls become pregnant in numbers disproportionate to those in the overall city population. The neighborhood as a whole is flooded with young mothers whose children will never experience what many of us regard as a normal childhood.

There is an old saying: "A nigga's between heaven an' hell, jus' like anybody else, an' still catchin' the short end of the stick." That adage holds some legitimacy as one considers the general condition of blacks in America as compared to their white counterparts. Boards of corporations as well as other enterprises continue to be run disproportionately by whites. Political entities have yet to resolve the dilemma of racial discrimination, a discrimination that perhaps can best be perceived with a glance at the unemployment rates. The percentage of blacks out of work is double that of unemployed whites. Some might argue that the problem is historic, that time will eradicate the vestiges of slavery that remain. Yet one is at times still inclined to ponder whether real integration has ever been the goal or whether another obscure exercise has been at the heart of the matter. And circumstances surrounding the Hill's redevelopment raise the very issue of just how much power blacks in America have had over their own destiny.

As late as 1982 seven acres of the Hill remained vacant. Twenty years after residents and businesses had been removed, redevelopment was still substantially incomplete. Currently, thirteen acres include two large office buildings, a supermarket, a restaurant, a fast-food franchise, and several small businesses. The ownership of these enterprises is overwhelmingly white. Could some of the black businesses that once existed on the Hill have prospered with selective renovation? Have the individuals who once lived there advanced comparably as the city has improved, or were they merely pawns in the game of progress?

In 1983 work on a federal court building was completed at the site of Vinegar Hill. Formerly residents of Charlottesville had to travel to nearby cities in order to have federal appeals cases heard. The newly constructed federal court building makes the handling of such cases more convenient.

Also convenient is the gigantic Omni Hotel, completed in 1985, which has already served as an attraction for many national and international conferences sponsored by the illustrious University of Virginia. With these new developments it is apropos to consider which of Charlottesville's citizens have been convenienced the most. And considering the developing prosperity of this rapidly growing town, it is critical to consider whether blacks who owned homes and businesses were adequately compensated for their loss of property in what now must be acknowledged as one of the city's prime real estate areas. If nothing else, one thing is certain. Neither black property owners nor renters were ever adequately compensated for the loss of their cultural center, a place that had somehow found a way to flourish in the midst of a citywide community that was repressive by its very nature of excluding blacks from important decision-making positions.

This book is a response to that repression, an effort to allow those who had no voice then to speak now with regard to how they felt about the urban renewal project and its impacts on the coming generations. Many of the respondents were interviewed in the early 1980s when much of the Hill remained vacant, 20 years after the initial demolition occurred. Quite naturally, some have concluded that a major objective of the city was to move the distinctly black neighborhood away from its place right beside downtown. Others have contended that the move was beneficial, providing modern facilities for many who previously had lived in a rudimentary rural fashion. This disparity of opinion provides the ultimate complexity surrounding this renewal project that took so many years to complete.

In our efforts to be as comprehensive as possible, we endeavored to record testimonies from as broad an array of people as possible: schoolteachers, businessmen, maids, and cooks, as well as quite a few others. What finally emerges is the picture of an American subsociety that functioned as an entity almost unto itself. Without access to secondary and higher educational institutions, many black parents sent their children out of town and sometimes out of the state to garner for them those advantages. As the struggle for integration grew into a national cause, the community banded together and pursued its own strategies against those who would perpetuate the status quo. The following is a testament to their determination against all manner of adversity and a tribute to what they were able to make of a community with severely limited resources in an era when equality was little more than a hollow catchword.

CHAPTER ONE

THE PRIME OF
VINEGAR HILL

In her 1933 master's thesis — "Charlottesville: A Study of Negro Life and Personality" — Helen Camp de Corse described the extent to which economic vitality existed in a small black community adjacent to the downtown district:

> The segment of Main Street lying between Fourth Street West and Preston Avenue, known locally as "Vinegar Hill," has forty-one buildings on the north side and sixteen on the south side. Of the latter only one is occupied by Negroes — the Paramount Inn catering to transients. On the north side there are both white and colored establishments. Here are barber shops, pool-rooms, stores for furniture, food and clothing, shoe repair shops, cleaning establishments, drug stores, fish markets, beauty shops, insurance companies, tailors, restaurants, etc. Much of this property is owned by Negroes. The largest building on the hill, the Coles Building, is owned by Charles Coles, a Negro building contractor, and occupied by a haberdashery, and a ladies clothing shop, a dentist, a physician, a life insurance company, a beauty parlor and a cafe. A number of other buildings are occupied by two or more businesses. Only one white establishment, a lunch room, is patronized by whites only, while one negro business, a barber shop, is patronized by whites only. All other white businesses are patronized by both races or by Negroes only. Some of the Negro businesses are patronized by both races and some by Negroes only.[1]

Just one or two generations after slavery had been abolished, a substantial body of black businessmen thrived in a small southern town. In assessing the prospects for such a situation, historians Leonard Broom and Norval D. Glenn, conclude that "the Negro businessman has several unique disadvantages, whereas white owners of stores and of many service establishments cater to all races, Negro businessmen, with few exceptions, can hope to attract only a Negro clientele. The potential clientele of the Negro businessman is relatively small and relatively poor."[2] However, Vinegar Hill was somewhat different.

Although most black businesses did have a black clientele, other black businesses served the black and the white community. And, as de Corse pointed out, at least one black-owned enterprise catered solely to whites.

Rebecca McGinness, born in 1892, and the wife of a prominent Vinegar Hill businessman, recalls that

Some of the property there was owned back to slavery times, when black people could first own property. Some of it was gradual from the white people moving out. I can remember when it was nothing but a pathway and Main Street was nothing but mud. And then they laid bricks. I can remember when they laid the first bricks on Main Street.

Of course, now Main Street is a well-paved thoroughfare that extends from downtown Charlottesville, past the top of the Hill, through the university, and out toward the woods of Albemarle County. Yet McGinness, herself a long-time schoolteacher, remembers the time when it was not even really a street and the town of Charlottesville was just as rural as those outskirts to which Main Street currently runs.

As we noted in our introduction, the stories of how Vinegar Hill got its name range from Irish legend to the story of a wagon, carrying a cargo of vinegar, being pulled by a team of dray horses. Edward Jackson, who was a waiter during the 1950s, offers the following account:

There is a history that everybody tells, that back when there were the old dirt and brick streets, a keg of vinegar fell off of a horse and wagon and broke. And from that, how do you say, aroma of the vinegar, gave it its name.

Lionel Key, an electric company meter reader on Vinegar Hill during the 1920s, had earlier attended school directly across the street from the southwest side of that area. Like Jackson, his story concerning how Vinegar Hill got its name centers around a container of vinegar falling from its wagon.

Well, I had heard several stories. The only one that I remember at the present time is that they said they were hauling vinegar up the hill on a wagon one day, and a barrel of vinegar rolled down the hill.

Drusilla Hutchinson, who lived on the Hill and worked as a cook in a private home, provides a variation on the type of cargo that was being transported:

Way back yonder in—have to go to the Good Book to tell you when it was—seventeen and something, was an old man, he had his wagon full of kegs of beer. And he was going up Vinegar Hill with them. And it came out of the wagon or something. And one keg of it rolled out and went down the hill. And he couldn't tell because it was against the law for them to be carrying it. And they say it was vinegar. And that's where they got the name from—Vinegar Hill. Rolled down into the bank, and they named it Vinegar Hill.

A native Charlottesvillian who was one of the first blacks to graduate from the University of Virginia provides this narrative:

There was a sort of a winery on Vinegar Hill at one time, and the winery was one of those kinds that used a lot of apples in making wine, and it smelled like vinegar. You know what cider smells like?

That same respondent, Booker Reaves, gives an alternative account with elements that resemble what others have said.

Well, there are several myths about it, and I don't know if anybody knows for sure. One was that before the turn of the century, when Vinegar Hill was more or less a dirt street, they had a trolley line, and it had mules pull the trolley up and down the hill because it didn't have the power to carry itself, and somebody said that somebody was hauling a load of vinegar, and it spilled, and the odor stayed there a long time, and that's why it's called Vinegar Hill.

Even if Vinegar Hill did originally acquire its name from Irish immigrants, one thing is nevertheless quite clear. Blacks, who later came to make up the vast majority of Hill residents, developed their own folklore concerning the matter.

From the time immediately after slavery until the 1970s, there were several basic types of black migration. Many blacks in the Deep South ventured northward, not necessarily to faraway places like New York, Detroit, or Chicago but just anywhere more "northern" than their homes in Alabama, Mississippi, or Georgia. In those instances, being able to get to Maryland, Virginia, or Tennessee was deemed satisfactory enough.

Many other blacks, who were already in the northern range of southern states, were satisfied just to get out of the country and into a nearby town. Hutchinson, for example, conveys the circumstances surrounding her move to Charlottesville.

I was born in the country, honey. I didn't come there until after I was married. That's going on now about—I ain't going to put that in there. Well, I lived in the country with my father and mother until 1933. My mother died, and then I went, stayed with my brother a while, and then soon as I could, got a house here in Charlottesville, found a job.

She elaborates further on the types of jobs that she held once she was in Charlottesville.

I took care of people, and babysitted, and helped people out in doing housework. I really loved what I was doing because I didn't have education to do nothing else. But like I said, I was a good cook. And a husband and wife's cook was off; I went and took her place and cooked and I always had enough for my son. We always got by. We never did have to move out the house because we didn't pay our rent. We just saved our money. And we paid our bills all the time. We didn't make much, but we never throwed away nothing, you know. We couldn't buy fancy stuff.... Then I worked in a beauty parlor. Back then, there wasn't anything for you to do but maybe work in somebody's kitchen or restaurants, you know, movies and things like that.

Hutchinson performed domestic labor and then moved on to work in a beauty parlor. Though limited in terms of formal education, she was determined to develop herself as best she could to better provide for her son. She is the essence of what is meant when it is said that blacks comprise some of America's most conservative people. With limited incomes, most had no access to luxuries but had to content themselves with a "pay as you go" mentality that often required them to pinch pennies just for their daily subsistence.

Though Hutchinson was a migrant into the Vinegar Hill area, other blacks were actually born there. George Ferguson, for example, the son of one of Charlottesville's first two black doctors, gives the details surrounding his birth in 1911 and his early childhood years.

I was born on 307 West Main Street, and that was right at the top of Vinegar Hill. I lived there for 13 years. I went to school at Jefferson Elementary School, and that is in the area that they call Vinegar Hill now, from the foot of Main Street and Preston Avenue up to South Street.

Then when they came with this urban renewal, from the foot of Vinegar Hill up to Fourth Street, down Fourth Street, down Commerce Street to the old Preston Avenue, down Fourth Street to Williams Street to Preston Avenue and back out to Preston Avenue as you know it now. It runs down by Fourth Street down to the McIntire Road. Prior to that time—the urban renewal—there were people who lived on Fourth Street, Commerce Street, from Fourth to Preston Avenue, people that lived on Williams Street, from Fourth Street to Preston Avenue, and people that lived on Page Street, from Fourth Street to Preston Avenue, and people that lived on Fourth Street out to Preston Avenue. When I was a youngster, people lived on Preston Avenue down by where Lane High School is now.

Vinegar Hill housed various types of businesses and residences. There were some stores down there. There were some barbershops. Then there were some residences.

And streetcars ran east and west on Main Street. It ran from what they call the lower station—C & O station—up to the university, one car did. And it turned around up there. At ten o'clock at night the streetcars used to come and back up into Ridge Street, and the car barn was right next to Mount Zion Church, and that's where they put them for the night. And the tracks ran up and down Main Street, and the little track out Ridge Street to the car barn.

The site that's known as the Midway site here at Ridge and Main—like they are getting ready to put up for houses—was old Midway School, and that's where the whites went to high school.

The black children did not have any high school in Charlottesville at that time. I can recall when my sister finished the eighth grade, my father had to make arrangements for her to go to high school in Washington. This friend of mine that you talk about, Mr. Tom Inge, there were nine children in that family, and his father often told me that if he had been able to send his children to high school here and the University of Virginia, he could have left his children a much larger estate than he did. But he had to spend this money to send all of them away to high school.

If you go down Fourth Street you will see the City Yard down there, and at that time it was the—Charlottesville had artificial gas, and they made this artificial gas from coal. People would go down there, and after they had used the coal, they had what you call coke, and they would use that for the fires and all.

City limits were not as extensive as they are now. In fact, the city limits have extended a lot in the last 25 years. As I said, I lived on Main Street until I was 13, and then I left here and went to Cleveland. When I came back, I had to go to Virginia State for school.

When Ferguson was a teenager in the 1920s, Charlottesville did not provide for the education of blacks beyond the eighth grade. Consequently, blacks as a whole were restricted in terms of just how far they could advance socioeconomically. Raymond Bell, whose father established the J. F. Bell Funeral Home in 1917, remembers:

Many of those families that lived in that area worked for the City of Charlottesville. That is, they worked in the City Yard. People on Williams Street, most of them worked over at the City Yard, trash collecting. Years ago when there were not indoor toilets, they had a truck that went around and would empty the outhouses. And blacks worked in those jobs—street repair, excavation, all kinds of work. At one time there was an incinerator right in the City Yard. Trash, all the trash in Charlottesville would be burned in that incinerator. Of course, they take that out now for landfill. But before, there was an incinerator. The other place they worked was at the university hospital. They worked at the school, doing domestic chores.

Most of them were, they were just janitors and just ordinary people, but they were, they were just ordinary people who loved people. They had no big jobs. You know what jobs around here are. I called them superiors because I thought they were great, and they always looked out for each other. They always looked out for us. We were children. They had no opportunity to have jobs like these kids have now. They didn't have an opportunity to even have a job—a decent job. See, I do everything, but they had, they didn't have it. It was not there. They didn't have the opportunity. See where I'm getting? They didn't have a living room like this. I've worked hard for this. My mother, my father—a home like this—they didn't have that opportunity. They worked, but they just didn't get that far. I'm telling it to you like it is. I can't speak for them because a lot of them are dead and I can't speak for them, but I know how hard they worked in the jobs they had.

Bell, himself an undertaker, explains how difficult it was for members of the generation before him to establish themselves in business. And the overwhelming majority of blacks did not even have that opportunity; they worked menial jobs and formed what was in essence a segregated underclass in Charlottesville. But as Bell observes, all those black workers should be deeply admired for their sacrifice and the bridge they laid down for other generations of blacks to use.

Black businesses on Main Street in 1917 (Courtesy of the Special Collections Department, University of Virginia Library).

Mattie Thompkins, who was only six years old when urban renewal transformed Vinegar Hill, also recalls how an earlier generation of blacks worked hard in spite of their humble occupations. Of her father, she states:

At first I believe he was telling me he was working at Leggett. I don't know for sure if he was a janitor or something. Whatever he was, he wasn't making anything but like seven dollars a week. And then from there he went to Chancellor's Drugstore, and he worked there for 27 years.

Thompkins, a telephone operator, goes on to explain the nature of her mother's employment.

Well, she was working, doing the best she could because she was doing like maid work, going from house to house, cleaning houses. That's about it—domestic work or whatever. There have been a great deal of changes, but like I say, when your mother and father were back then and that's all they knew how to do, and that's all they could do, and then when modern times came—progress—it was too late for them to do anything because they had aged. And like I say, if they didn't have a college education or just a regular education with a diploma, then where would you go but doing the same thing?

Once again, we are informed with regard to how lack of opportunity kept blacks from holding certain types of jobs. Thompkins is diplomatic as she conveys the employment circumstances of her mother's generation. The interviewee is all but on the verge of giving praise to what she calls "progress" and "modern times," when, to put it quite bluntly, people should never have had to suffer simply because they were born into an earlier era. The "regular education with a diploma" to which she refers is the high school degree that her mother could never have received in Charlottesville because there was no high school available for blacks to attend. And her mother certainly could not have gone to the University of Virginia, which did not admit blacks in any significant numbers until the latter part of the 1960s, and did not admit women until the early part of the 1970s.

Another respondent, Alexander Scott, describes the social condition of Charlottesville blacks during the 1940s and 1950s.

Any person or groups of persons who labor over a generation or generations and develop whatever they can develop by the sweat of their own brow may not be able to build castles—and more often than not, they aren't—but I have a feeling that whatever they build and whatever they take care of and whatever they own is on the plus side for any person or for any group of persons or for any neighborhood.

Some of those people who lived in Vinegar Hill and worked on two jobs and three jobs, at a low cost, many of them did the very best they could. And you can't say that that person was shiftless. He's living in an economy that he just couldn't work it out because he had not kept up with the skills and whatnot. And 30 years ago or 40 years ago, about the only employment black people had was the type of employment which you could classify as domestic. And domestics have always been poor, particularly when it was done primarily by blacks, because we had a philosophy of patronage, I guess. People grew up, they had not completely liberated themselves. We had some of the leftovers from a much earlier age, even back to slavery.

Listening to Scott speak, his voice softening at times, one hears a certain measure of despair. When Charlottesville did finally provide high school education for blacks, Jackson P. Burley High was one of the early schools, and Scott became the principal. His extraordinary mission was to figure out a way to engender real progress in spite of the limited opportunity.

Historians August Meier and Elliott Rudwick evaluated the national employment situation as it existed during the few decades just before legal integration. In assessing the difficulties, these two distinguished scholars declared that "[be]cause of white prejudice and discrimination the overwhelming majority of free Negroes were unskilled laborers. Negro entrepreneurs found it difficult to obtain capital, since lending institutions considered them poor risks. White businessmen were reluctant to employ Negroes in skilled or white-collar work. Where employers were willing to hire a black, white laborers often refused to work with him."[3]

Often the only work available for blacks was work that no one else wanted. Laura Franklin left Charlottesville in the 1920s to attend high school at Hampton Institute. But in those days scholarships for blacks were extremely limited

Vinegar Hill resident going to work in the early 1960s.

in terms of how much money was allotted per student. When her money ran out, Franklin was forced to return to Charlottesville to the same type of work that the previous generation in her family had done.

I lived with my aunt and she was tight, and I had to work and try and take care of my money. But she was working up there and she asked me if I wanted to—while I was at home with the children so small, the students asked me, the students wanted somebody to wash for them. So, she asked me if I wanted to wash, take it and I wash them at home. And I washed for some students instead of up at that lady's house. And I also worked years before with my mother. And then that lady kept me working for her off and on.

In referring to her aunt as someone who was "tight," Franklin is essentially reiterating how socioeconomic circumstances demanded financial conservatism. The tenuousness of those economic times for blacks in particular is evinced most profoundly as the interviewee explains how once money was no longer available for education, her "safety net" was employment as a washerwoman for university students and other whites in town.

In recalling the period before 1926, when there was no secondary education for blacks in Charlottesville, former barber Frank Henry confirms that

It went as high as eighth grade, and during my time, you had to stay in the eighth— you stayed in there two years. And when you left there, you had to go out of town to get a high school education.

Ruth Coles, the daughter of another Vinegar Hill barber, reiterates:

Jackson P. Burley High School, which blacks attended before integration.

Well, the school over there, the school that I attended as a child has been demolished. But it was over there on Fourth Street, right across from King's. And it only had eight grades. And when you finished those eight, that was as far as blacks could go in Charlottesville. You had to go some place to a boarding school for your high school education. Then when I finished the eighth grade here, I went to Petersburg to what was then known as Virginia Normal and Industrial Institute, having changed hands from Virginia Collegiate. And of course now, you know, it's Virginia State University. I finished Normal School there in '21. And after I had taught four years, I married and stopped teaching for nine years. Then I went back to teaching again. When I went back to teaching, I also went back to school. My oldest daughter and I graduated from college together. We were the first to do that at Virginia State.

Yet another person, Walter Jones, who for forty years lived in a section of Charlottesville adjacent to the Hill, describes the educational situation:

If a family was lucky and their children could go to school and finish high school, then there were colleges that they could go to. There weren't mixed colleges. You couldn't go to white colleges, but there were colleges that they could go to. And that happened in many instances. I never did go to college though….

When Jefferson was first built, it was just the eighth grade, but when Jefferson did add the twelfth grade, see I went to Albemarle Training School. Albemarle Training School was a good trade school. That's where I went to school at. I didn't go to a city school. At that time Albemarle County School had better credits than Jefferson did. Jefferson didn't have as high credits at that time as Albemarle Training School did.

August Meier has traced the history of industrial education in America as pertains to its institutional origins for blacks:

> The Freedmen's Bureau commissioners and missionary school teachers, many of whom were familiar with the idea of manual labor schools from their abolitionist days, pushed forward the cause of industrial education. Thoroughly imbued with the importance of the values of thrift, industry, and morality, they believed it their duty to inculcate these values.... As early as 1864 and 1865 various societies established "industrial schools" where trades such as sewing and shoemaking were taught.[4]

By the 1880s Booker T. Washington had made industrial education famous through the vehicle of Tuskegee Institute. What the Freedmen's Bureau and missionary teachers had begun in the 1860s, though, actually wound up being a crucial beginning, providing some type of "advanced" education where, for blacks, there had formerly been none. In addition to such trades as shoemaking and sewing, brick masonry, carpentry, and plastering were taught. In black schools throughout the South, extensive training in those fields continued, sometimes for over a century, well into the 1960s.

In 1963 Raymond Bell became the first black person ever appointed to the Charlottesville School Board. And in that capacity he clearly understood the history of black education in Charlottesville and the monumental task that lay ahead in terms of enhancing educational opportunities for blacks.

When Vinegar Hill was in its prime, there was no black high school here. So, when the blacks would come out of elementary school, they would go to—For example, my mother went to Virginia State College to go to high school. They had a high school at Virginia State. So, she would go there. They went there for two years.

Bell explains further what the options were for those Hill residents who were determined that their children have high school and college educations:

Hartshorn, which became a part of Virginia Union. Manassas had a training school. Manassas, Virginia. So, your blacks had to go out of the city to get a high school education.

It wasn't until around 19—Oh I suppose it was 1924, 1925, that they had a high school which was a part of the Jefferson Elementary and Jefferson High School. So, you didn't have blacks going to high school. The Inges—the Inge children—none of whom went to high school in Charlottesville because they came along in a generation where there was no high school. Yet their parents knew the value of education, and they would send them out of town to go.

I suppose it was difficult, but you had a very large percentage of blacks that were going on to college. And when I came along—I finished high school in 1944—60 percent of my class went on to college. And that happened all along that way because

The old Jefferson School (Courtesy of the Charlottesville Department of Community Development).

although the kids were poor, they could still go to school. They had a kind of an open admissions policy. You'd go to Virginia State. If you wanted to go to school then, you could scrape up enough money. Parents paid monthly. They paid the room and board on a monthly basis. So, it was rough, but at the same time there was a great awareness that kids needed education. Blacks had to get education. And that was the thing. "Go to college, go to high school, go to college," that type thing. So, you had a very unusual percentage of blacks going on to further education, advanced education, some of whom didn't finish college, but they went.

And there was a school at Christianburg. That was another place. The man who did the renovation on this funeral home went over to Christianburg to take up a trade and learned carpentry and came back and opened up. Charlie Coles is a graduate of Hampton Institute, the man that I mentioned about having a contracting business. He built this building here that you see. He built this. This was built by black contractors, 1927.

Some residents, like the Bells, Coleses, and Inges, understood the value of secondary and college education, and they were in a position to pursue those goals for their children. But Bell, in his assessment, has embellished the reality somewhat. It would be good for us to temper that glowing account of the past with the hard sociological observations of Elliot Liebow, who admonishes us:

> It is essential to keep in mind that we are not looking at men who come to the job fresh, just out of school perhaps, and newly prepared to undertake the task of making a living, or from another job where they earned

> a living and are prepared to do the same on this job. Each man comes to
> the job with a long job history characterized by his not being able to sup-
> port himself and his family. Each man carries this knowledge, born of his
> experience, with him. He comes to the job flat and stale, wearied by the
> sameness of it all ... terrified of responsibility — of being tested still again
> and found wanting.... It is the experience of the individual and the group;
> of their fathers and probably their sons. Convinced of their inadequacies,
> not only do they not seek out those few better-paying jobs which test
> their resources, but they actively avoid them, gravitating in mass to the
> menial, routine jobs which offer no challenge — and therefore pose no
> threat — to the already diminished images they have of themselves.[5]

Liebow was writing in the 1960s about an inner-city corner frequented mainly
by black men whose circumstances can best be described as desperate. Such a
situation had to have been worse than that of the upper echelon blacks of
Vinegar Hill, even in the 1940s in a small southern town like Charlottesville.
But somewhere in between Bell's and Liebow's assessments lies the reality of
what the human response is to the persistent racial oppression that has characterized so much of our history.

Charles Johnson, a black man who unsuccessfully sought the Democratic
nomination for Charlottesville City Council in 1960, expresses a view similar
to Liebow's:

*Back in those days, the idea was prevalent among blacks that you didn't need so much
education, that your position in life would be just a human beast of burden, services
in one way or another. They felt that you didn't need any more education at that
time.*

Johnson's and Liebow's comments make clear the phenomenon of class divisions
even within the black community. Although there were blacks in Charlottesville
who could afford to send their children away to school, others were not financially able. It was mainly this latter category of individuals who were either
unemployed or locked into menial jobs with no opportunity for advancement.

Sociologist J. Wallace Jackson analyzes how blacks in general have suffered
from socioeconomic exploitation:

> Since slavery, Afro-Americans have been relegated to the status of a resid-
> ual element in the American occupational structure. The black labor force
> has been functional in the American economy because it suited the flexi-
> bility of labor that is necessary in the shifting economic conditions of a
> capitalist economy. During periods of recession, blacks can be ejected
> from the labor force, and during periods of economic expansion the reserve
> of black labor can be drawn upon. But to be effective, the system must keep
> from blacks the realization of the actual role they are playing in the per-
> petuation of their own exploitation.[6]

During its prime, the Hill itself stood as something of a symbol against the
very exploitation to which Jackson refers. It was a part of town where at least

some degree of black advancement and prosperity was extremely evident. Then came urban renewal, and as black newspaper editor Sherman White points out,

It removed a symbol. While it wasn't much, it was all that we had. So, it took away the image of blacks in business, the importance of blacks in decision-making positions. Not just because they're black, but because there are other blacks looking at them. And my kids coming up, if they never see their father do anything but janitorial work—I'm not saying there's anything wrong with janitorial work—but if that's all they ever see me do, that's all they may ever aspire to.

In 1926 a high school curriculum, substantially industrial, was added to and housed in the same building as the all-black Thomas Jefferson Elementary School. It was not until 1951 that a distinct high school (without the elementary and middle school grades) opened its doors for blacks. Located just a few blocks north of Vinegar Hill, it nevertheless posed a bittersweet situation due to the town's segregational stance and the limited employment opportunities that the students of that generation would continue to face even upon graduation. Still, Alexander Scott, who became principal of Burley in the late 1950s, is able to boast:

Our classes were very seldom less than 100 in the graduating class. It went from 97 to 130, 135 as I recall. And quite a number of the students that we trained did find employment in the community. For instance, we had a very good course in business at that time. Probably eight or nine or ten units of instruction in business education. Consequently, a considerable number of those students went into the area of distribution—salesgirls, marketing, and stockroom clerks, secretaries, and semiclerical duties and things of that sort. You see, these doors at that time were opening up a bit wider, and we trained our students and placed them in the areas.

Nursing, brick masonry, and college preparation were other very successful programs at Burley during Scott's tenure. In addition, as Sherman White declared, black-owned businesses were a source of community inspiration. Ferguson, the owner of a funeral home near Vinegar Hill, avows that

There were some fairly nice black businesses that existed. Such things as cleaning and pressing establishments, shoe shops, barbershops, beauty parlors, insurance companies, grocery stores. Sum total was at 20 businesses at the peak. At least that many.

Though students who were enrolled in the business curriculum at Burley had little expectation that the general Charlottesville community would welcome them with open arms, the city was on the brink of social change. It was change by inches, a case of blacks moving more and more out of basements and backrooms into more visible employment positions. But the work still was usually menial, and most blacks entering the job market had to be satisfied, as had generations of blacks before them, with the knowledge that their efforts would only provide them with basic needs and perhaps provide their children with a bridge toward something better. A crucial feature in the midst of those circumstances was the existence of black enterprise on Vinegar Hill, which stood as yet another possibility, an alternative avenue that some blacks could pursue.

Edward Jackson, who was born across the street from the north end of Vinegar Hill in 1922, gives an account of businesses that existed in the neighborhood:

There were a couple of white restaurants in the Vinegar Hill area also. There were black-owned barbershops that catered to white trade in the Vinegar Hill area. Mr. Pollard was right in that area where Inge is, but a little further east. In fact, where the General Electric building is there, Ron Martin building, Pollard was in there— Ol' Man Pollard. And, of course, there was a family of folks.

Frank Henry—they ran a barbershop. And I reckon ol' Frank is pushing, you know, getting up in his 70s. He's still living, yes. Saw him not too long ago.

Ray Haskell ran the Hampton Shop. That was for cleaning and pressing. Collins ran the shoe shop—Collins' Shoe Shop. That was one of them. Carroll Tonsler—before Carroll Tonsler, my father—they had a drugstore there on Main Street. And that was Dr. Jackson and my father. There were several of them. They had formed this investors group—small corporation. It was a very nice drugstore. But I was quite young back then, and I don't remember it too well. But then after that failed, my father put in the restaurant, poolroom, and beauty parlor upstairs and what have you. And then after he let it go, Carroll Tonsler, who went in there, was very successful and made a nice buck.

There was Mr. McGinness. That also was another tailor shop. Mr. Edwards ran a sort of retail outlet, and used clothing store and whatnot like this. There was a Southern Aid Insurance Company that was there. They owned that building. And Henry Bell was there in recent years. He ran a retail store. Of course, you already met Mr. Inge. And then there was a fellow—Carter—ran a very nice restaurant down there. He was a cook on the C & O Railroad, and he opened up a real nice restaurant. Who else? Then they had a guest hall across the street that the Fergusons ran. They weren't related to George Ferguson.

Then there were the Coleses. They were also, he was a builder, and he had his establishment and whatnot down on Vinegar Hill. The Coles brothers—Willie and Charlie Coles. They also had—their home was there, along with the Wests' home. The Coleses and the Wests. They were very, very substantial citizens, both of those families.

Perhaps Jackson recapitulates the history of black businesses so well because of the business legacy within his own family. As a young man, he watched from close proximity as his father continued operations at an outdoor advertising establishment that the elder Jackson's uncle had bequeathed. Originally begun in the 1880s, it was at one time the only outdoor sign business in the entire United States.

Meier specifies that "from the late 1880s there was a remarkable development of Negro business—banks and insurance companies, undertakers and retail stores."[7] This might seem an anomaly during a period so shortly after slavery; however, there were quite a few blacks possessed with the necessary business acumen. Edward Jackson's brother, William, points to an additional factor—the particular need, during segregation, for blacks to render services to one another.

The insurance business has done a good job as far as blacks are concerned. And they came in existence at a time when people could not get insured by other companies.

Bell notes further that

As far as the businesses were concerned, most of the black businesses there in the Vinegar Hill section were, I would say, kinda small businesses. You had a cleaning, pressing shop, shoe shine, restaurant, and there were a number of funeral homes in that area—funeral homes that moved out. Small shops, small businesses. But they still were making a living. They didn't want to move out. Man named Tonsler had a poolroom and restaurant and perhaps had the most profitable business. My brother had a grocery store there on Vinegar Hill, and he had to move. His name is Henry Bell.

Although most of the businesses were small and service- or trade-oriented, they were essential to residents of Vinegar Hill. Thomas Inge, born in his father's grocery store right there on the Hill, reflects:

The greatest thing I liked about, remember about Vinegar Hill is all that business there. There was the undertaker, Mr. Bell. J. F. Bell started his place on Vinegar Hill. My grandmother had a boarding house on Vinegar Hill. Another man, Mr. Joe Watson, had a shoe cobbler's shop—a shoe repairing shop, they call it now—on Vinegar Hill. Mr. George Jones had a restaurant on Vinegar Hill. There were cleaning, pressing establishments—two of them—on Vinegar Hill. There was our store, which was on Vinegar Hill. And John West, the very wealthy black man, lived on Vinegar Hill.

Black boarding houses, such as the one owned by Inge's grandmother, were common during the early part of the twentieth century due largely to the fact that equal housing was not available. Those blacks who did own homes, though still segregated from the white American mainstream, represented a relatively new social order. Most blacks, however, had to rent either houses, floors, or separate rooms. Raymond Bell offers himself as an example.

I was renting a house from a man named Jackson. And he had a little house there with two bedrooms, $50 a month rent. My wife was teaching school, and I was working at the funeral home, making about $50 dollars a week. It was an ideal place to rent, starting off married life....

Mr. Jackson was a black man, and his grandmother, a woman named Nannie Cox Jackson, owned approximately 40 percent of all the land in the Vinegar Hill section. She was a very enterprising black woman who was a home economics teacher in the high school. And she went around buying up real estate. So, a lot of the young

*teachers—young couples getting married, getting started—could always rent a place
from Mrs. Jackson or from her son. W. E. Jackson was the son of Nannie Cox Jackson. And when she died back in 1963, she had an estate of over a million dollars.
That's a black woman.*

History has informed us of black entrepreneurs such as Maggie L. Walker of
Richmond, Virginia, and Madam C. J. Walker of New York City, the former
a banker and the latter an innovator in hair-care products. But in small towns
all over the South, there were Nannie Cox Jacksons who prospered with very
little notoriety outside of what was given them in their own relatively isolated
locales.

Rebecca McGinness, who was born in Charlottesville in 1892, also
remembers when

*We didn't have a hotel. We had boarding houses. We didn't have a hotel, and we
couldn't go to the hotels here. But people had boarding houses and rooms. People
roomed around whenever they could.*

Blacks were not allowed to stay in white hotels, so boarding houses were the
primary substitute. And some Hill residents even opened up their own homes,
leasing rooms to accommodate the housing need while earning extra money.

Lionel Key, who delivered newspapers on the Hill from 1918 to 1920, has
his own vivid memories of a vibrant community.

*There were many black families located there. There was a church. In fact, I believe
there were two churches: one on Commerce Street, the other one on Fourth Street,
across from the Jefferson School.*

*The Jefferson School was a black school, located on Fourth Street between Com-
merce and Brown Streets. That was the old building. It's not there now, but they
expanded, added to it, built, in addition, a new building and continued to use it for
many years. They finally tore down the old Jefferson School. The later building is
now used for school offices. That's located on Fifth Street, northwest.*

*From on Main Street across on Sixth Street, in still the same general area, there
were black families. I believe that it was a black undertaking establishment on Sixth
and Commerce Streets, operated by Mr. Bell. His sons continued with the undertaking establishment and now operate it from that location.*

*On Sixth Street there's also a black Baptist Church that's in operation now.
Across from the church for many years—I don't know who was originally at that
location—Mr. William Jackson, the local owner of the signboards, the billboards
we called them. There were many other good black families living in the area. And
on Main Street, at the beginning of Sixth and going on down Main Street to Vinegar Hill, there were few if any black families between Sixth Street and Fourth
Street.*

*On the corner of Fourth Street, northwest, was a Model Laundry that was
operated by Mr. Yokum who lived on the opposite corner of Fourth and West Main.
And on the north side of Main Street, the east side of Fourth, was the Inge Grocery*

Store, operating, I remember it, back for many years. And his son continued to oper-
ate it until, within the past, maybe the past year, not too many months ago. Next to
the Inge store was a vacant lot. Then there was a black barbershop for black people.
Next to it, I believe, was a black shoe shop and one or two small black businesses.
Then Mr. West—I believe his name was John—was a black barber that operated a
white shop down in the main part of the city. His son continued to operate that
for many years after his death. Then across Third Street was Dr. Ferguson's home,
a black physician. Next to that, I believe, was an Italian food market, a fruit mar-
ket, and then across from what they called Mason's Alley was a shoe repair shop run
by a black man. He had mostly white customers, but some black, of course. Next to that
was Poindexter's Drugstore, run by a white man. Then a white confectionery store,
a grocery store, a meat market belonging to the area. Then, I don't know how far back,
but right close to that, I don't believe they had any other businesses between that.

There was a building that was later operated as a drugstore by black people.
That was not in business too long. And, I believe, after that, Mr. Carroll Tonsler,
a black man, operated a pool hall and maybe several other concessions in there. He
owned the building, living quarters above. I think he lived there for a while. I'm
not sure if he lived there until they tore the building down. But then, going on down
the Hill, next door, was a Greek confectionery store. Beginning at about that point,
I believe there was a black barbershop, for blacks, run by Bill Barnes. Then right
along in that same general area, one of the fraternal groups, I believe Masons, had
their offices upstairs in the building. And there were one or two other black busi-
nesses there. And then, another building that many years ago was operated as a black
poolroom. Finally, McGinness, a tailor, a black man, took over and operated a tai-
loring shop there. And there was a George Carr that ran a clothing store, primar-
ily men's, I believe it was. He was in there for a long time. And then from that point
on down, I don't believe there were any more businesses—black businesses—on that
side of the street.

Across on the corner of South—between South and Main Street, up on the high
bank and next to the fire station—was a dwelling that black people owned, and I
do not remember the names of the people who lived there at the time. I remember
the people, but I don't remember who owned it. It seems to me they may have been
connected with the Jacksons who had the billboard service.

In addition to homes and businesses, the Hill provided other important
social functions. Raymond Bell acknowledges that

We had all kinds of black neighborhoods per se—Preston Heights, Rose Hill Drive.
But Vinegar Hill, believe me that Vinegar Hill was probably more identifiable, was
the more popular. It was the fact that that's where the blacks were concentrated in
terms of entertainment, and you had a Masonic Hall there. The Masons met there.
And they had dances on Vinegar Hill. So, that was the place blacks identified with.

There was a place called Odd Fellows Hall. Now Odd Fellows Hall was not
in the Vinegar Hill section. But it was right on the border line of Vinegar Hill. The

Raymond Lee Bell

Odd Fellows Hall is still in existence. And that's right above the Vinegar Hill Theatre. Right next to it is the old Odd Fellows Hall. The black Elks Home is right around the corner from Odd Fellows Hall. So, when I was coming along in the '30s and '40s and '50s, all the black dances were held at Odd Fellows Hall. That's where everybody would have them regardless of what club you were in. My father and mother would always go— If they were going out to a dance, you knew they were going to Odd Fellows Hall. That was the only place we had that black folk could have a dance. So, they went there. And then they later built the Elks Home, which is around the corner from there. And the Elks Home had a restaurant in it. So, that became a kind of a center for black recreation and entertainment.

Commenting further on the social life, George Ferguson recounts:

They had all the fraternal organizations, I guess you'd call them. Masons, Eastern Stars, Elks, Odd Fellows, Knights. And people became members of those. People were more interested in churches than they are now. They had programs not only in the regular Sunday service, but they always had morning services, evening services. They had young people, they had BYPU, that was maybe around before the night services started. That was where the little boys and the little girls used to meet and walk home with the girls and that type of thing. Then they had night service. Quite a few people worked as domestic help. They were domestics, and they couldn't go to the morning service. So, a lot of the churches were well attended at night. They had entertainment at the churches and all types of— Some of them were fund-raising for the church, some of them were just entertainment. They were, more or less, culture. They had people that would stand up and read Paul Laurence Dunbar's poems, and recite other poetry and musical entertainment and that type of thing. They also had federated women's clubs. Those are still in existence. Different clubs like Phillis Wheatley and whatnot that women belonged to, and they had their programs and entertainment. They generally met in the homes. Men would congregate in the barbershops and discuss politics, discuss all the phases of life, whether it was safe to ride in an automobile, and who ain't go'n ride in an automobile.

Many memorable social events, usually racially exclusive, occurred on Vinegar Hill. And then there were city-sponsored events such as the Dogwood Festival

Parade with its floats and school marching bands winding through the downtown area. Thomas Johnson, who lived on the Hill for seven years during the late 1950s and early 1960s, tells of the excitement he felt as a boy.

I guess it was the parades that always fascinated me there. The Apple Festival, Dogwood Festival, and all these festivals where they used to have those parades, which used to be very great. Used to couldn't wait to get there.

For a whole century after the end of the Civil War, Vinegar Hill was indeed the center of Charlottesville black cultural life, a self-supporting community comprising many who endured and sometimes prospered in the face of cruel adversity.

CHAPTER TWO

ADVANTAGES AND DISADVANTAGES OF URBAN RENEWAL

On January 28, 1960, an article titled "Businessmen Endorse Vinegar Hill Project" appeared in the Charlottesville local newspaper, the *Daily Progress*. The Charlottesville Redevelopment and Housing Authority had devised a plan whose major objective would be "elimination, through total clearance, of a slum, blighted and deteriorated area adjacent to the Charlottesville central business district."[1] The newspaper article reported that the local chamber of commerce unanimously voted its approval of that plan:

> The Charlottesville Redevelopment and Housing Authority's plan for redevelopment of Vinegar Hill was endorsed yesterday by a joint committee of the Chamber of Commerce and the Retail Merchants Association.
>
> With fourteen of its sixteen members present, the joint committee unanimously resolved to "approve the plan of the Charlottesville Redevelopment and Housing Authority for the redevelopment of Vinegar Hill area and such public housing projects as may be necessary in order to carry out that plan."[2]

What had become of Vinegar Hill in the years between its prime and the beginning of the 1960s? Ferguson offers this assessment:

You had restaurants to open up and close down, open up and close down. That was on Main Street, that section of Vinegar Hill. Now, behind Vinegar Hill, they were all, more or less, residences. Those residences that people complained about, most of the properties were owned by whites renting to blacks, and a lot of them had outdoor toilets. Do you know what that is? They didn't have water in the homes. They had faucets out in the yard. I forget what they called them—iron faucets out in the yard that you turn the water on and get your water.

Some of the nicer residences that I recall in the Vinegar Hill area were on Pres-
ton Avenue where Lane High School is now. Blacks lived on one side of the street,
and whites lived on the other, and they had, they came up to Fourth Street. But those
were taken over by eminent domain—the city—when they built that Lane High
School back down there in the '30s.

The renewal came about, and any time you have anything that is disrupted,
there are a lot of people who don't like it. But we lived at a time of change. I would
say that the majority of those homes were properties that were rented, and the few
nice homes that were there, I imagine that the people were satisfied with them. But
the whole area was a blight.

By the time urban renewal had become a major issue for debate in Charlottesville, quite a few residences and even some business structures on Vinegar Hill were substandard. The Hill's prime was indeed over, and there were
those in the neighborhood who were becoming less and less able to keep pace
with the developing urban economy.

In an address presented to the March 25, 1960, meeting of the Charlottesville Council on Human Relations, out-of-town analyst John P. Murchi-
son specified particular issues as being paramount to the local black problem.
Among other things, he stressed: "It sounds like your problem is not a housing problem; it's an economic problem due to wages.... You ought to see about
getting those wages up."[3] The *Daily Progress* furthermore reported:

> Murchison said housing conditions described here made it sound as if
> city officials should be asked to enforce a minimum housing standards code
> as was done in Washington.
> Charlottesville officials have drawn up such a code, but it has never
> been adopted because of a feeling that it would eliminate low-rent hous-
> ing needed by low-income families at a time when housing for this income
> group is considered in short supply.[4]

Perhaps another commentator — an unidentified, Charlottesville real estate
broker who was also present at that meeting — best conveyed the condition of
certain inner-city blacks.

> "Many of the families now living in what have been termed blighted
> areas — such as Vinegar Hill — pay a nominal rent of only about $30 per
> month but actually pay far more than this because they have to buy
> firewood and pay other expenses that would often be covered in one lump
> rental payment.
> "Families that pay $10 per week rent often would balk at paying the
> same amount if it were collected on a monthly basis."[5]

Each of these various assessments points to a socioeconomic disparity between
blacks and whites, as well as to a disparity between wealthy blacks and those
blacks who had to struggle for mere subsistence.

The trends of black employment during the late 1950s and the early 1960s reveal a national attitude that has been characterized by sociologist Charles Silberman as plain and simple "corporate bias." Silberman maintained that "In the South, of course, discrimination is conscious and overt; employment of Negroes is limited by the tradition that Negroes not be permitted to work on an equal status with whites, and that they never be placed in a supervisory position over whites."[6] Having evolved from the even more sordid past of racial discrimination, most blacks correctly assumed that white businesses would continue to discriminate. And the consequent attitude among those blacks was often, as Elliot Liebow has argued, one of wishing to avoid the inevitable rejection and to settle instead for menial types of legitimate employment.

Others earned income through participation in illegal activities. Felonious crimes were not common, however. Instead, the bulk of crime included socially acceptable illegal activities such as "bootlegging" and "numbers running." William Jackson explains the latter phenomenon:

Numbers games were going on then. There were numbers played at barbershops. Not by the barber necessarily. If you did, that was just part of human nature. I play Bingo at the Safeway because I hope I get that thousand dollars. So, people played numbers because they wanted to be lucky. Hopefully they'd be lucky and they could get some money easily.

We have seen in recent decades how individual states have exploited that aspect of "human nature" to fill their administrative coffers. But long before the advent of statewide lotteries, places like Vinegar Hill offered the means for satisfying the persistent desire on the part of some citizens to gamble in hopes that their lives would suddenly change.

In the midst of the larger Charlottesville population, the Hill was a subsociety within which frequent interaction and interdependence were the norm. Former Hill resident Alies Jones remembers:

They were very nice people. I used to could cross from my yard to somebody else's, and somebody'd holler across their yard to me. And we'd borrow wood and coal and stuff like that from each other. Them was the good old days then. Like, if I needed some coffee or something, you could go into each other's house and get it.

Another former resident, Sadie Mason, speaks yearningly:

It was nice. I enjoyed it. Nice people. Very congenial. They looked out for everybody—the children, the adults. Very congenial. And so, they took it all from us. We had to go some place else. And I was a little girl then. I'm talking about when I was a little girl. Friends looked out for us, and we was just neighbors, that's all, neighbors. We looked out for each other.

Ruth Coles adds that

We families were a great thing when I was growing up. We spent a lot of our leisure time in the neighborhood. Neighbors were close. And we didn't have parks, we didn't have playgrounds. We owned that vacant lot over there, and as I told somebody the other day, I said, "We had mini-parks before ya'll ever knew what mini-parks were," because we had a flower garden, played croquet, and ball, and, as I say, the whole neighborhood, we played together. Then, we had house parties. Lots of times we had them here in our house, or we'd go to the houses of our friends. And our parents were very liberal. We could have them as often as they thought wise, and that seemed to have been quite often enough for us. Then, we had a lot of activities in our churches. Then we went in for plays and things of that sort. I think our leisure time was well spent and enjoyed. And, of course, in those days, all over there where City Yard is now, was just one great big vacant place, and we had lots of snow when I was a child. All the friends and neighbors had lots of fun over there coasting. And down in the bottom, there was a branch, and the boys over there were ice skaters. And we thought we had very good childhoods.

Booker Reaves, a student and then a principal at the Jefferson School, contends that

Even though there were different economic levels of black people who lived in the Vinegar Hill area—some had better homes than others—they were all very closely knit, and they were people who were helpful to each other in times of stress, and they were people who would come together and work with people all over town. I know. I lived, as I told you, in the Ridge Street area, and my parents had lots of friends in that area, and I had friends out there.

Interestingly enough, however, Walter Jones is of a different opinion:

Do you want the real truth? Blacks ain't never been closely knit, not unless something comes along now, because that's why the Caucasian race has always been able to get over on them, get over and do anything they want to do, whenever they want to. Because blacks never really could stick together. You know, they never had the love for each other and that type of thing. A curse is on the black people, in a way of speaking.

Notwithstanding this most intriguing perspective, virtually every other respondent insists that there was a very strong sense of togetherness. In fact, Coles remembers the occasion when a new doctor arrived in town and was awestricken by the closeness he witnessed among the members of the various black classes.

One young man who came here after I was grown came here to practice medicine, and he said that this was the first place that he had ever been where cooks and physicians and dentists and everybody seemed on equality. But that's the way we grew up. We didn't have class lines. Of course, most of the blacks who were not in business for themselves were employed at the university or by some wealthy person, and their standards of living were set by their employers. Of course, their employers might have had something that cost thousands of dollars, and the employee had something that only cost a few. But they still had that same lifestyle.

The extent to which class lines were or were not rigid is debatable, but the sense of community was, of course, stronger when the Hill was fully functioning with its varied assortment of residents. Connie Brooks, a former member of the University of Virginia housekeeping staff, recollects that

They were closer than they are now. People were more helpful to each other at that time. Because of segregation, I guess, they would go and take food. Everybody would go and take a basket or something like that. They would help each other. We would go every morning and knock at every door and see how everyone was.

Although the Hill comprised different economic classes, most of its residents were eager to help others, especially in times of crisis. Still, by 1960 the question of whether to use the mechanism of urban renewal to upgrade the area had become a widely discussed and controversial issue. Months before a final decision was to be made by the city, the matter dominated the local news. Using data provided by the Mayor's Committee for Public Information on Public Housing and Urban Renewal, the *Daily Progress* published the following summary of the advantages and disadvantages.

ADVANTAGES OF URBAN RENEWAL

Slums. Urban Renewal will eliminate slums where neighborhood conditions and dwellings have become detrimental to health, safety and morals, and where the social and economic liabilities so greatly outweigh the assets that rehabilitation is neither practical nor feasible. In an average city, slums account for 33 per cent of the population, 45 per cent of the major crimes, 55 per cent of juvenile delinquency, 50 per cent of arrests, 60 per cent of Tuberculosis victims, 50 per cent of disease, 35 per cent of fires, 45 per cent of total city service costs, and contribute 6 per cent of the tax revenues. No current data on these matters are available for Charlottesville. Earlier studies made by Committees working on these matters developed information for Charlottesville that indicates a similar pattern.

Financing. When a community desires to undertake Urban Renewal projects with Federal assistance, it must contribute its share of the project cost either in cash or in the form of local grants in aid — such as public facilities and improvements. The Federal contribution may amount to as much as two-thirds of the net project cost.

Rehousing. There must be a plan to facilitate the rehousing in decent, safe and sanitary dwellings for all families displaced by Urban Renewal and other Governmental activities. Under the provisions of Section 221 of the National Housing Act, the FHA can insure loans on liberal terms for new or rehabilitated low-cost private relocation housing anywhere in the community. Eligible for this housing are new families in the Urban Renewal area or those displaced by any other type of Governmental activity.

Preference for admission to new or existing low-rent public housing is provided for displaced families of low income. The Public Housing Administration, a constituent of the Housing and Home Finance Agency, upon application of the local housing authority, and with the cooperation and approval of local government, can contract to make development loans and pay annual subsidies for public housing projects, within the maximum number of units authorized by Congress. The proponents of Urban Renewal advance the following arguments:

1. Fine stores and sparkling downtown districts
2. Wide streets and plentiful parking areas
3. Pleasant parks, apartments and office buildings

4. Reduces the number of slum areas in the city
5. Provides for orderly renewal of wornout and obsolete areas
6. Furthermore, it minimizes overcrowded conditions:
   More traffic congestion
   Dwindling business
   Outmoded buildings
   Disorganized use of downtown property
   Falling property values
   Soaring civic costs

DISADVANTAGES OF URBAN RENEWAL

Government Interference. History reveals that Governmental assistance has been accompanied by, or has in effect constituted, Governmental intervention. Some degree is understandable, once the decision has been made to assist. The Government, no less than a private investor, desires an accounting of its funds and must establish rules designed to lessen the risk.

Housing Laws. Our Housing Laws, initiated during a period of general economic depression, are regarded by some as incompatible with current conditions.

Public housing is administered to the Redevelopment and Housing Authority under the State laws governing such operations. Contracts and agreements made with the Federal Public Housing Authority must be honored.

Who Pays for Public Housing. The local property tax payer and the U.S. Income Tax payer pay for public housing. The tenants of public housing pay rents based upon their income. Each family is required to pay not less than 20 per cent of its income for rent, including utilities. Only in rare instances has this covered the full cost of operating and managing the low-rent projects.

The Cost of Public Housing. The Housing Act of 1949, as amended in 1956 provides that the cost of building and equipping dwelling units cannot exceed $2,500 per room except in high cost areas where it may be as much as $3,000, for elderly people, excluding the cost of rent and normal dwelling facilities. The size of the units varies within each project. The average is two bedrooms, but a few have four bedrooms.

The Federal Government's Increasing Role. The Federal Government has been assuming more and more responsibility for housing and housing policies. If local and State Governments took more initiative in originating and carrying out the necessary programs, less interference would be forthcoming from the Federal agencies. With public housing, as with free public anything, there is always a tendency to increase the number of persons eligible to benefit and to expand the area of authority.

The Moral and Social Effects of Public Housing. There is evidence that public housing is characterized by a confusion in its basic objectives, that it has fostered restrictions upon the earnings and initiative of its occupants, that it has deterred the production of rental housing by private industry, and that it has permitted the growth of power hierarchies, in the form of public housing management. The claims of the public housers that public housing eliminates slums, that it houses low-income families who could otherwise not afford decent housing, that it reduces crime, juvenile delinquency and other antisocial behavior, are questioned.

Public Housing Tenant Morale. In public housing projects, there is a rule that tenants' income may not increase more than 20 per cent over the income earned at the time of acceptance when income and employment are steadily rising, incomes inevitably increase if the tenant is ambitious. Thus, if his income exceeds the amount set by the Authority, the tenant either hides the fact, or his wife withdraws from the labor market, or he has to move out. These are harsh choices. There have been instances where occupants of housing projects refused overtime work and promotions for fear of being made to vacate their project home.

Slum Clearance No Justification for Public Housing. Research indicates that a substantial number of persons whose total income appears adequate to allow them to live in homes that most people would consider standard, prefer to allocate their income in such a way as to minimize their outlay for housing. As is also shown, many people prefer remaining in what are widely considered to be slum conditions, rather than to live in public housing projects that carry with them restrictions and disruptions of long established customs and relationships. Even in circumstances where slum clearance is essential or inevitable, it is said to be erroneous to conclude that public housing necessarily provides an acceptable solution.

Juvenile Delinquency and Public Housing. Supporters of public housing frequently base their appeal on the relationship of substandard housing and slum dwellings with a high instance of crime and delinquency. These contentions do not reveal why some of the families living in slums or other substandard dwellings do not possess the social ills which reportedly contribute to the living conditions. For that matter, they do not explain why one boy in a family may be incorrigible, while his three or four brothers, living in the same environment, are not. Where social behavior is concerned, the effect of public housing is difficult to determine.[7]

In the midst of this controversy, Mayor Thomas J. Michie submitted to the *Daily Progress* the text of a speech he was to make on the evening of June 10, 1960. In that speech he urged support for redevelopment on the Hill and lower-income housing projects for residents who would consequently be dislocated. The following is excerpted from the mayor's appeal:

> This city has been talking about public housing for 30 years, as evidenced in an item a few days ago in the Twenty Years Ago column in The Daily Progress. And the matter has been actively before City Council off and on for 10 years. Urban renewal is a comparatively new thing in the country at large and the motivation and driving force back of our project at the beginning was simply to provide decent housing for people who were then — and still are now — living in sub-standard homes....
>
> Now sub-standard is a technical term. It does not mean just below average; it means houses that are really not fit to live in in this modern age. It means houses with no running water in the house, with outside toilets, with inadequate heat, light and ventilation or in a really dilapidated condition.
>
> If you have any doubts about the existence of such houses just take a walk through the area back of Vinegar Hill where most of these houses are to be found and your doubts will disappear.

Now, if you want to be hardboiled you may ask, "Well what is that to me? I don't have to live there and the people who do live there don't have to live there." But those people do have to live there. There is nowhere else for them to go, much as they would like to. If you doubt it ask any real estate man to find you any vacant Negro housing in Charlottesville.

Furthermore, you cannot escape this problem by saying that you are not your brother's keeper. For conditions like this affect the entire community. Slums breed disease, crime, and juvenile delinquency. That is a well established fact....

There are very few cities the size of Charlottesville that have not gone in for public housing, and for the same reason. It is the only way in which the slums can be cleared.

In the State of Virginia, every city of Charlottesville's size except Petersburg has public housing, and many smaller cities such as Bristol, Harrisonburg, Norton, and others have also found it desirable to resort to public housing. In the 16 Virginia cities having public housing, 14,500 housing units have been built....

Now up to this time only public housing had been under discussion and little attention had been paid to the possibility of urban redevelopment. About this time, however, some one had the idea that not merely the worst slum houses back of Vinegar Hill should be torn down to be replaced elsewhere by good public housing, but that the whole area should be converted into a fine, modern business area, an extension of the downtown Main Street area which was blocked from moving in that direction by the existence of this slum.

I cannot conceive of anything that would give the downtown area more of a shot in the arm, for the downtown area will be a great boon to the entire city.

Perhaps most of you do not realize that there is no residential area in the City of Charlottesville that pays enough taxes to pay its share of the total cost of running the city government. It is the business areas, largely the downtown Main Street area, which pay the taxes that carry the lead for our government.

From a financial point of view as well as from a social and cultural point of view, the substitution of a fine modern business section for the slum area now existing back of Vinegar Hill would be the most forward looking step that has been taken in Charlottesville in many, many years.[8]

Financially speaking, Vinegar Hill was a burden to the city of Charlottesville. Some sections of the Hill had minimal property value, contributing very little to the city's tax base. Furthermore, although many of the property owners paid the taxes that were assessed, many others did not.

The part of Vinegar Hill that was "dilapidated" posed a dilemma for the adjacent and more prestigious downtown area that was mostly white-owned. With a heritage of plantation labor, there were blacks on the Hill who continued to engage in farming activities that reflected that historical background. In addition to growing their own vegetables, many residents of the Hill raised chickens, pigs, and cows. Some sought merely to provide their own subsistence whereas others sold their produce and livestock to local grocery stores.

Substandard houses on Vinegar Hill in the early 1960s.

A number of citizens in Charlottesville were greatly offended by conditions on the Hill. Some members of one white, middle-class organization, upon viewing the details on projector slides, were absolutely alarmed. Gene Arrington, the director of the Charlottesville Redevelopment and Housing Authority at the time, describes how "They couldn't believe it. They could not believe it! Chickens right there in the middle of our city!"[9] Mayor Michie argued that instead of such conditions existing in the central part of town, Charlottesville — through renewal — could one day gain the benefit of an extended business district. Additionally, the mayor made an appeal to the consciences of the white majority. He depicted the poverty that existed on the Hill and maintained that every American citizen, even those heretofore neglected, had the right to a decent standard of living.

Sociologist Andrew Billingsley has even gone so far as to argue that American society owes its black individuals a very special debt. The condition of poverty — suffered by so many black generations — was not merely an unfortunate quirk of fate:

> Let the average middle-class white person who reads this contemplate the following: Where would he be today and how well would he be able to meet the needs of his children if his parents before him, their parents, and his ancestors for four hundred years in this country had been (a) forced to

work without pay, (b) prevented from learning to read and write, (c) prevented from moving about at will, (d) prevented from living together as man and wife, and (e) constantly told in ways more effective than words that they were inherently inferior? Culture is cumulative. Special efforts to indemnify the Negro people are not a matter of guilt price or charity, they are a simple matter of back pay.[10]

Billingsley declares slavery to be the cause for the generally lower economic status of the black race in contemporary times. And he further asserts that white oppression is a disadvantage that has yet to be overcome. One hundred thirty-five years since the abolition of that "peculiar institution," blacks as a whole have yet to gain economic parity.

As has already been mentioned, for many decades blacks migrated up from the Deep South into northern states. Simultaneously, blacks left the rural settings of Virginia to settle in the towns and cities of that same state. Most of those individuals sought economic opportunity to replace the systems of exploitation — first slavery and then sharecropping — to which they had hitherto been subjected. However, their arrival during the latter half of the 1800s in those towns and cities provided little more than what most of them had had before. Stark discrimination in education and employment was to be the standard practice for more than half of the following century, and consequently, disproportionate levels of poverty continued to be the national trend. While the country as a whole was progressing, most blacks were left far behind. Upon studying the housing situation of blacks in general during the time that renewal in Charlottesville was becoming an issue, Bernard J. Frieden concluded that

> The rate of improvement in housing during the 1950s and the extent of the remaining problem make it clear that the goal of a decent home for every American family is still far from achievement....
>
> While the migration continues, an important task for public policy in the big cities is to help the poor find decent housing. When the poor are Negroes, the problem takes on an additional dimension. It is evident from the experience of the 1950s that housing abandoned by the white middle classes in their move to the suburbs has not been reallocated equally to Negroes and whites.... Racial segregation, as well as poverty, has limited the housing gains of Negroes in metropolitan areas.[11]

What prompted the move to the suburbs? What indeed are the causes of voluntary segregation? Whatever we conclude, it must be acknowledged that Frieden made a quite valid point in assuming the correlation between societal segregation and the resultant insufficient housing for blacks. Furthermore, as one considers the historical background and the governmental priorities of the time, one thing becomes abundantly clear: Renewal in some extensive form was an inevitability for the residents of Vinegar Hill.

CHAPTER THREE

HISTORICAL BACKGROUNDS

Housing Conditions on Vinegar Hill before Urban Renewal

The Housing Act of 1937 was the first piece of United States legislation that allowed for federal subsidizing of local housing programs. Congress, by that time, had perceived the need to eliminate accommodations that it felt were unsafe for human habitation. Local housing codes in general date all the way back to the days of Hammurabi, who ruled the city of Babylon approximately 2,000 years before the birth of Christ. Indeed, practically every civilization since then has devised health and safety standards for the dwelling places of its members. The difficulty, however, has come in the execution of those laws. Authors Thomas Johnson (not the former Vinegar Hill resident), James Morris, and Joseph Butts, in analyzing the situation as it existed in America during the late 1950s and early 1960s, concluded that "extended neglect by the cities has caused blight to develop and spread, slums to be created and vast areas of many cities to fall into a state of decay. In short, the failure of cities to renew themselves on a continuing basis has caused them to accumulate large quantities of worn-out and out-moded structures and facilities."[1] Much of the decay that existed on the Hill by the late 1950s and early 1960s can be attributed to just such municipal neglect, a lack of concern about the conditions under which blacks had to live.

Bell had mentioned that Nannie Cox Jackson was the owner of substantial amounts of property on the Hill. Teresa Price, Nannie Jackson's granddaughter, contends that

If that land now were under city ordinance—current city ordinance—it wouldn't be up to code and probably would be considered a hut. But at that time, she had no problem renting in there. It was all airtight and safe and with adequate sewage and

Housing inspector visits homes on Vinegar Hill in the early 1960s.

that kind of thing. I think she got five dollars a month from each house, or some-
thing like that. That was good for that time. She managed that very well. Now, those
people that were displaced were another problem. Where did they go? I can't remem-
ber that far back, but that was the problem—those people finding a place to go. And
I suppose most of them did go into Westhaven. I can think of one or two families
that did go into Westhaven. All of them didn't go into Westhaven.
    We'd already had a lot of experience with eminent domain because we'd already

been routed out of the area where Lane High School is and landed in this bind. Lane High School went in before Vinegar Hill. So, we lost property where City Hall is, where Lane High School is, where Vinegar Hill is, where Jefferson School is. We just stay on the fringe of the redevelopment all the time.

Thomas Johnson, whose family had to move from their 14-room house on the Hill when he was 13 years old, asserts that

I think it was a good move. The buildings weren't kept up well at all. And a lot of them were dilapidated and just needed demolishing. I really was glad for the move.

Let me see, I must have been about nine, and they had this huge explosion down at the gas plant down the hill there. And one man got seriously hurt and all this stuff. And we were about two houses from there. And that was one reason I was glad to move from that particular area. They had this gre-a-a-t, long—I guess it was longer than this house across—there was this huge tank where they used to store gas at. And as a matter of fact, it was sitting next to the school. Yeah, it used to sit right next to the school. It used to frighten you, because my classroom, when I was in the fourth grade, was right next to it. That was the thing I didn't like about it there generally. And plus the noise. 'Cause we used to have a lot of public trucks and all that stuff and city trucks and everything going through there.

Mattie Thompkins declares that

The places were rundown. And like when it rained, it poured because everything leaked. You had to put pots under the—I mean down on the floor in order to hold the water. When we did move to Hardy Drive, it was a change from wood stoves. I was at least, I believe, six years old because that's when I was going to Jefferson.

To varying degrees, these three respondents point to the reality of urban decay. The dilemma, however, concerned what exactly should be done about the situation in light of the fact that not every structure on the Hill was dilapidated.

On June 14, 1960, a city council election was held in Charlottesville. As part of that election, voters were also "asked to decide whether the Charlottesville Redevelopment and Housing Authority should be granted powers to continue activity, and whether the authority should be given permission by Council to proceed with redevelopment on Vinegar Hill under a Federal Urban Renewal program."[2] The sole Republican nominee supported renewal. On the other hand, the three Democratic nominees were divided in their opinions of how the potentially explosive Vinegar Hill situation should be handled. Democrats Bernard Haggerty and Lindsay Mount supported redevelopment — the clearance of Vinegar Hill and the removal of most of its inhabitants to a low-rent public-housing project eight blocks west of the downtown district. Controversy resulted as few of those on the Hill agreed with the prospective move; and much of the antagonism that resulted was due to the distrust that most blacks in Charlottesville had with regard to the city's white administrative officials.

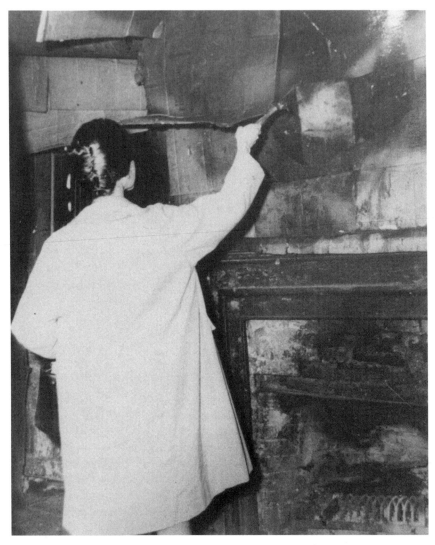

Another inspector assesses one of the substandard homes on Vinegar Hill.

The *Daily Progress* printed the views of candidate Mount:

> Mount says adoption of the authority's program would mean "we can make a good start on a new westbound street and a connection between Ridge Street and McIntire Road, both urgently needed to help solve our growing traffic problems. It means we can get rid of unsanitary conditions which seriously menace the health, not only of the people living in the area, but of all with whom they come in contact; and it will remove a potential fire hazard which endangers large areas of valuable property nearby."

Mount says the charges by opponents that the housing projects would become slums themselves "are false and misleading."

He says the same charges have been advanced in almost every city where the programs have been proposed. "And, almost without exception, as housing units are built and slum shacks begin coming down, the opposition fades away and is replaced by citizens' groups dedicated to helping the authority rebuild other decayed areas."

He says that those opposing the redevelopment and housing program "have no confidence in the good sense of the people or in the leadership of those elected by the people."[3]

It would not be appropriate to blame the city entirely for the dilapidated conditions that existed in some places on Vinegar Hill. Much of the blame should be directed at those slumlords who allowed their properties to depreciate to dangerous levels. But as Teresa Price avers, some rent payments were so low that landlords could hardly be expected to pour that money back into housing maintenance. In looking at the dilemma, one gets the view of a lower socioeconomic class of people who could not afford much else and came to expect very little.

Yet one wonders to what extent Mount really cared about the poverty-stricken black people who lived on the Hill. Half a decade before the 1965 Voting Rights Act, how likely was it that those particular people would be able to turn the tide of an election? When he talked about a "leadership ... elected by the people," he referred to a leadership that was entirely white. Who were "the people" to whom Mount deferred, trusting in their "good sense"? And who was he mostly concerned about when he spoke about the traffic problems and the need to "get rid of" unsanitary conditions?

The Struggle for Integration in the Public Schools

In *Plessy v. Ferguson* (1896) the United States Supreme Court upheld a Louisiana statute stipulating that public facilities for blacks and whites would be separate.[4] The Court concluded that "if he be a colored man and be so assigned (to a coach), he has been deprived of no property, since he is not lawfully entitled to the reputation of being a white man." Pursuant to that ruling, numerous state legislatures enacted new laws enabling localities to keep the races separate in practically every social situation.

It was not until the *Brown v. Board of Education* decision in 1954 that the Supreme Court eliminated that "separate but equal" philosophy with regard to public facilities.[5] However, in spite of the court's reversal the most decisive battles were yet to be waged. Years after *Brown* had been handed down, southern localities continued to deny the equal access that the court had officially mandated. Raymond Bell expounds extensively on the history as it pertains to Charlottesville in particular.

The "Byrd Machine" in Richmond took a stance on the desegregation issue when the courts struck down school segregation. The state government took a stance of mas-sive resistance, that they would resist this. And they waved the banner of states' rights. And there was a case, court case, in Charlottesville where—it was called Allen v. Board of Education. And that went on through the various state and fed-eral courts, and it ended up over in Harrisonburg with Judge Paul. And that's a very interesting era, especially because we had Spottswood Robinson, Oliver Hill, Mr. Tucker—Sam Tucker came on later. But we took that case on—Allen v. Board of Education. And it was named after the first black child. His name was Ernest Allen, who now coaches basketball. But Ernest was young at the time, and his parents entered him. So, it was Allen v. Board of Education.

So, as a consequence of massive resistance, the Charlottesville schools were closed. They closed down all the schools. And the black kids went to private homes to be tutored. My sister, who was a teacher in the public schools, was one of the teachers that taught. I remember Ronald and—they were twin boys—Ronald and Robert, I think. They used to come here, and Olivia Ferguson, the daughter of George Fer-guson, who was the president of the NAACP at the time, insisted on going to Lane High School. And they didn't allow her to go, and she ended up going to a little tutor-ing class up at the school board office on 14th Street right next to Venable School.

So, you had this area of massive resistance. Kids out of school and then, of course, Judge Paul ruling that schools would be desegregated. And you had the mayor of Charlottesville, named Judge Michie, who is the father of Tom Michie, just elected to the office of the Senate in Richmond, his father was mayor. He had been a lawyer and a military governor overseas in Italy during the occupation. And he was mayor and he issued a proclamation saying that anyone that would interfere with the orderly process of desegregation would be arrested. And he meant it. He meant any-one. And, of course, that was a warning to the white citizens actually. So, the first day of school was a big deal here, you know, kids saying, "Well, the blacks are there." Some white parents kept their children out. And there were, of course, problems.

So, Charlottesville was one of the first schools in the state of Virginia to reopen. And that's an interesting part of history. And Olivia got her diploma from high school, not in commencement exercises, but just from that local office. So, it was inter-esting. I, having been on the school board, was asked, before a civil rights commis-sion one time, "How was Charlottesville able to desegregate its schools so much faster than other places like Prince Edward County?" And my answer to that commission was that it was because of Allen v. Board of Education. We went through the courts and I think the NAACP selected Charlottesville as one of the test cases, to spearhead that whole effort. They concentrated on Charlottesville. And Judge Paul issued an order that the schools would be desegregated, and they were.

And then, of course, that meant the phasing out of Burley High School, which was a joint consolidated school of county and city blacks, only blacks. You see, Bur-ley High School was a black high school, and you had black kids coming from the county, being bused, and Charlottesville school kids going to Burley. They walked to school, and county kids were bused there. So, that school was phased out after the desegregation law. And the black kids went to Lane, and the county black kids had to go to Albemarle. So, it was that process of evolution in terms of civil rights.

Now, on the other front, we—of course the NAACP was very active in that case of schools, but we were hitting employers at the time. We had an interracial commission here headed by a man named Henry Edwards, who was president of a local bank. And I served on that commission along with three or four other black people, and our aim then was to get desegregated facilities—restaurants—even at the Holiday Inn North. I remember going there with Mr. Williams, and I walked in and the head waiter said to me, "You know, we don't serve blacks here, but you can eat here," not knowing that I was a black. Looking at me, he wouldn't know. So, I told him we would be there, so we were. We ended up sitting in at that Holiday Inn a couple of days, and they desegregated. And several other places. There was a little place called Buddy's. He closed his restaurant, which is now on Emmet Street right across from Cavalier Motel, where you see the AAA. That was Buddy's Restaurant, and we went up there, and a man by the name of Henry Johnson, Reverend Henry, fought him. H. Floyd Johnson was the minister of Zion Union, and it was at that location that Reverend Johnson was jumped on by some huge man, some white guy who attacked him physically to try to break up the marching, the protest march. And we didn't let that deter us. We kept coming back, and he closed down rather than to open his place at that time. So, that was the only one I remembered where there was physical violence. But on the whole, it was a bitter pill, and they were reluctant to swallow it. Things happened.

We were going to sue them. They knew that they were going to be. For example, we had some very well-meaning white people who went to some of the restaurants up on The Corner and talked with the owners and so forth: "Why don't you open this place up to your black students here at the university?" And they went along. They went along with it. It gradually worked out that we weren't going to give them any disease by them associating with us. But they were—It was tradition, you see.

After the schools were desegregated—The NAACP deserves a great deal of credit for that. That was the one, that organization was the only mechanism that made things happen locally. Of course, you had the civil rights marches going on in Selma, Alabama, and all over the country. Things were happening.

And there was another phase where we attacked the segregated housing in Charlottesville. We wanted a fair housing rule. And we would go out on Sundays and go to white developments such as the one off of Cherry Avenue—Johnson Village. Going over there, and they didn't want to show us any houses. Reverend Bunn was very active in the housing phase. He is with the First Baptist Church, and he's stepping down this year. He's been there 36 years. He was the founder of the local NAACP branch here.

Mrs. Bunn was the first black in charge of the Health Department, the visiting nurses there. She was a pioneer in that. They live in the county, some ways out. So, you had developments moving toward desegregation in terms of housing, schools, employment, and the public facilities.

An interesting chapter on the University of Virginia Hospital. At one time all the blacks were in the basement of an old ward in the hospital. And we brought Spottswood Robinson and Oliver Hill here. They talked about it. Mr. Randolph White was probably the top black there. He did all the hiring of black people, black orderlies. And Randolph White was very active. He's the man who's the editor and publisher of the Charlottesville-Albemarle Tribune. They wrote the director of the hospital, saying that all the blacks would strike if they didn't move the patients. So, we prepared to file the suit because it was a state facility.

They were able to desegregate that black ward in one day. They moved all the black patients up to the wards, and the problem they ran into, although the administrator and policy makers made the policy, we ran into the problem of people who were ward nurses who wanted to maintain segregation. They would put blacks with blacks. They wouldn't integrate the wards. So, we had to go back and threaten them again with a lawsuit. So, the administration sent out a memorandum to the effect that if you blocked this, you'd lose your—you'd be fired.

So, you had a problem there, getting the so-called line folks, line staff to go along with what their superiors wanted to do. You had to fight that all the time. I remember when one of my children, my second son, was born there, they were saying that they had no room on Barringer for my wife who wanted a room and could afford a private room. They wanted to stick her in some little nondescript room without a bath. So, they left her without a bathroom. And, of course, knowing blacks who worked there, I was able to make one phone call, and I found out what room was vacant on Barringer. I went to the director and told a man named John Stacy, who was director, if he didn't give her that room then I would sue him. Within an hour, she was in the room. So, you had to do all those kinds of things. You'd threaten people with suits, and it was a difficult thing.

We were willing, were going to sue them, and they knew it. We meant business because where the blacks were, there were pipes dripping, rats, all kinds of—I remember going through a hall, they actually had people out in the corridors—blacks because they wouldn't put them upstairs in empty rooms. This is before the desegregation. This type of thing can be repeated all over the South. And you're paying your money. They're charging you as much as they charge everybody else. And you'd walk through that hall downstairs there in the basement, and blacks would be lined up in beds there, very sick people in that type of environment.

So, you had the hospital. And, of course, you know the history on the University of Virginia. They had a fellow named Swanson who applied for law school. He was admitted. He didn't finish, but he won admission to law school. And Booker Reaves got into the School of Education, and I think Booker was the first black to be graduated from the university. But they went very slowly, screaming and carrying on, shouting and screaming before they would. But the reality of politics, these politicians would come to the black community and you would tell them, give them some demands: "If you want to get in office, you're going to have to do some things." So, we were able to effect change through the political process. And we still need to do that. It hasn't happened yet. Because you only have to look in the city hall in terms of blacks. You don't even have blacks where you need them, county or city government where we can make some decisions.

I'll tell you what happened with it. Like it happened all over the country. Apathy set in. And you had people saying, "Oh boy, we've made it." But the truth is, we ain't made it. We're far from it, and it just breaks your heart to go to NAACP meetings now. You don't even have enough members. Sometimes half a quorum. And I, along with some others, have been out there thirty years with the NAACP, and we don't have young people coming along. And some of these people who have enjoyed the fruits of other people laboring to bring about change are so damn comfortable in their jobs, they don't even come out. And I'm speaking of school teachers in particular who make pretty good money. You have to drag them to get them to join the NAACP.

I think it's worse now in terms of—There's so much more we've got to do, and unless we can get into the economic mainstream, well, we can say, you know, it's nice to be able to stay in Hilton chains and all this business. But it takes money. And you still have blacks not making the kind of money that whites are used to. And I frankly am really disturbed about the apathy of blacks. We still have many blacks leaving Charlottesville after graduation, going to Washington, Baltimore and other places, when they should stay here and try to do things here.

Before the mid–1920s, those blacks who were financially able to move from Charlottesville to a city that provided high school education for them, usually remained away. George Inge, who founded Inge's Grocery on the Hill on July 1, 1891, used his enterprise to ensure that each of his children would be able to go to high school and college. Bell explains further:

Now, Mr. Inge, who was a merchant there, had eight children. And all of them went to college. Two of whom became physicians. One became principal of a school in San Antonio, Texas. Another one became a Ph.D. in chemistry at Hampton Institute. One of the daughters taught the third grade—Miss Gertrude Inge. Three of them were schoolteachers, the girls.

Having left Charlottesville for educational advancement, one of the sons, Thomas, did return, whereupon he inherited the family business. This second-generation Inge reflects:

Well, I was born in the Vinegar Hill neighborhood. I'd been living there until after I married, and then I bought this place. That was in 1942, I believe.

My mother, my father, and all of my sisters and brothers were born there, and they moved out. I came from a big family. There were about nine children—three sisters and five brothers, and myself made six boys.

They all moved away. See, at that time we didn't have a high school here. They went up to St. Louis to attend high school because my father had a brother out there, and after that, they all went to the University of Minnesota, where they went into professions—two physicians and one went into real estate, and one went into the teaching field, but she didn't go to St. Louis. She went to Hampton. The rest of them—I believe all the rest of them—went to St. Louis. I was next to the baby. I have one sister younger than I am.

George Ferguson's father, a Howard University Medical School graduate, chose to uproot his entire family so that his son could get a high school education. That Ferguson son depicts the circumstances:

There was no high school for blacks in Charlottesville, and my father had planned to move to Cleveland before my mother died. So, he followed through with his plans so he could keep the family together. We lived in Cleveland, and after he decided to come back to Charlottesville, I went to New Haven. And when I came back here from New Haven, then I was ready to go to Petersburg to school. So, he was here. But I was in school in Petersburg. Then after he died, I lived in Richmond. Washington was really my second home. I attended school, and my mother was from Washington, and her family lived there. Then, of course, after working in Richmond, I went to school in New York.

George Ferguson expounds further on the phenomenon of blacks leaving Charlottesville not only for better educational opportunity but also for greater employment opportunity.

We didn't have a black high school until about 1926, and this caused a lot of young people to just move on out, and they went away. Families were—take for instance a child who ranges around fifteen—as the old saying goes, once you go away from home, you don't ever come back. A lot of families were separated that way. Grass always looked greener around the cesspool, so they stayed away. And the job situation here is not very good. Because Mr. Jefferson, people in Albemarle County and Charlottesville never wanted any industrial plants. So, we don't have any industrial plants or that type of thing. Highly skilled—Sperry, Stromberg-Carlson—that have come in recent years. Job opportunities are not as great as they could be, and people moved on.

Blacks during that era could advance only so far. Slavery had been the institution that put shackles and chains on previous generations of blacks, binding them to the slaveowners and the land. Now second-class citizenship was keeping many blacks locked in a distinctly different type of economic bondage.

Even after the high school grade-levels were added in 1926 to the Jefferson School, further educational limitations prevented those black graduates from attending anything other than segregated industrial and "normal" schools. Those who qualified for admission to the state's white colleges were—in lieu of being allowed to attend classes there—given the funds to attend school outside the state. In comparing those days to the 1980s, Thomas Inge says that

Everything was separate. Schools all separate. And I never dreamed that Negroes would be attending the university like they do now. I just thought that would never happen. I just thought that was something that would never happen.

George Ferguson (Photo by Rick Copeland).

Some Negroes were very successful barbers. Two brothers had a barbershop. And then they used to work out at these fraternity houses. What blacks did, they, you know, did the work there—janitor and clean up at these fraternity houses, and that was about all they did. Shined shoes and that sort of thing. They worked in the University Hospital as orderlies. They've always done that. There were no black nurses up there, of any kind. And the black doctors, they don't even—we don't have any right now, here in town.

Connie Brooks, who went to New York to attend high school before returning to the housekeeping staff of the University of Virginia, remembers how, upon her return in 1964, she was surprised to see integration gaining a foothold.

I was shocked because I used to go in the drugstore, and you couldn't think of ever sitting down, even to have a Coke. And my sister came down with, she brought her two kids. We went just to get, you know, to get sodas. They wouldn't serve us. That was in the beginning of the sixties.

When I came back, I was shocked. I really was, and I said to my friend, "Oh gee, what are they sitting there for?" I saw all these black people sitting in the Five & Ten, and I said, "Oh, why are they sitting there?" She said, "Oh, you can sit down there now."

Honestly, I still couldn't believe it. It was such a change. I just couldn't believe it. So, I'd never seen a black person sitting. And if you went in the Five & Ten, and if you went to a restaurant and wanted some food, you would have to go to the back of the restaurant and eat it there. They'd have a little window, and he'd put it in a brown paper bag and hand it to you. That's the way it was.

Brooks goes on to describe how segregation was strictly enforced on buses and other forms of public transportation.

We had to sit in the back. I don't care if every seat was empty in the front, you still had to sit in the back.

The *Brown* decision provided the basis whereby not only schools but also other public facilities could be integrated. Yet the various levels of Virginia government mounted a well-organized campaign to prevent *Brown*'s implementation. The governor and virtually all of the state legislature immediately opposed integration, and they were able to garner overwhelming white citizen support. The call went forth for "massive resistance," which in essence represented a last-ditch effort to maintain separatism and thus whites' superior position in society. However, the NAACP chose to use the Charlottesville public school system as a test case. NAACP lawyers joined with Charlottesville black citizens to take to court, once again, the issue that the highest court in the land had already decided in their favor.

George Ferguson, president of the local branch of the NAACP during that time, tells about the delays, the frustrations, and the local lawsuits that had to be filed to breathe life into the *Brown* decision.

I was elected president in 1955. The Supreme Court decision was May 17, 1954. And then in 1955, the Supreme Court ruled, "With all deliberate speed." And we filed our case in 1956, with the plaintiffs in with the NAACP lawyers, going back and forth in court and fighting and so forth.

Then in 1958, we'd been going to court, back and forth, federal court. First it was here. Most of these hearings were in the summertime, so the federal Judge Paul said we didn't have air conditioning in this court over here, so he had us over in his court in Harrisonburg. And in the fall—and, of course, during this time massive resistance had come about—the general assembly had ruled that if any blacks were assigned to a school district, the school district would have to close.

Then in 1958, my daughter was a senior in high school, and she was assigned to Lane High School as a senior. There was another little fellow, John Martin, who was assigned to Lane High School in the ninth grade, and some of the children were assigned to Venable School.

In early September 1958 several black students were assigned to the previously segregated white James Lane High School. Those students were selected on the basis of which black families could afford to be the most supportive for the duration of the educational experiment. Ferguson continues:

That was all worked out between the attorneys, and they were also picked out, I think, on the stability of the parents—that you would stand up and not backtrack. We had all this schooling with the NAACP lawyers. At that time, Spottswood Robinson—Richmond—and Oliver Hill were the principal lawyers. Plus, the leadership was from the national offices. Thurgood Marshall, and there were other lawyers.

Success did not come easy. Sherman White, a student at the time, explains how his attempt to desegregate was unsuccessful.

Well, I was one of the twelve original plaintiffs that tried to get into the Charlottesville school system. While I was unsuccessful in getting in, I think we paved the way for those that did get in. And I think it's only fair to say—this was in the late '50s—I think it's only fair to say that initially, when it happened, there was an awful lot of turmoil.

In the '60s there was a thing called massive resistance. This is when those people in authority, the governor on down, said that they would resist and encourage the people to resist any form of integration, and this is where you had Prince Edward County come up in the news where they closed the schools down. And there was a lost generation down there, didn't even get to go to school. And the other thing that grew out of that that was very bad, I thought, was the tension, the unnecessary tension. The leaders of the state were saying, telling the citizens to willfully disobey the law. And fortunately, because the NAACP at that time was very strong and very well organized, it was able to bring a lot of pressure to bear legally and turn these things around.

Charlottesville public schools closed, and parents of white students resorted to organizing "little private schools"—mostly in churches and individuals' homes—to provide for the continuation of their children's education. Meanwhile, the families of black students who had been assigned to white schools were also prepared. Refusing to allow their children to return to all-black schools, they continued their demands for integration. With white schools closed, the school board found itself in the rather precarious position of having to hold classes in the superintendent's office for the handful of black students who, by now, must have felt like they were simply pawns in a series of political games and compromises. Ferguson declares,

This was all a long, drawn out process. It didn't just happen here, here, here. We had these hearings in court. Then the city, I guess, spent a million dollars fighting, or more.

And so, these two schools were picked out because Venable School was more or less—at that time children who belonged to university faculty members attended that school. That's on 14th Street. Lane High School was the only white high school in the city, and my daughter and this other little fellow had to pass Lane High School to go to Burley. And these children that were assigned to Venable more or less lived closer to Venable than they did to old Jefferson.

So, they were picked on where they lived, and then when the judge assigned

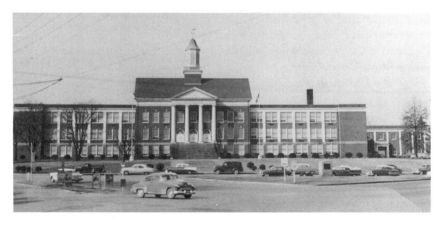

James W. Lane High School, which was adjacent to Vinegar Hill but was not open to blacks until the late 1950s (Courtesy of the *Daily Progress*).

them to the schools, then the schools would close. They closed in September of '58. They stayed closed until February.

The school board was mandated by the state of Virginia to close the schools. The governor came on TV and all this type of thing. Lindsay Almond was the governor then, and he came on TV. Then the NAACP had to go back to court to prove that massive resistance was unconstitutional, which they did. And in February they had gotten that through. It came through in January. So, my daughter was out of school, and the other children.

And the white children that were out of school, the whites got together and set up classes in the Elks Home and churches and residences and so forth, and the white teachers went on and taught. Then the discipline got so bad, they wanted me to have some of our children to go to see if they could be admitted to these schools, knowing that they would be closed. And, of course, I had to stay abreast of everything, and I knew what was going on, and I knew that they wanted us to go in there because they wanted to close those schools because of the discipline.

These little private schools. See they had them in churches and Elks Homes and different buildings around, and they would teach. Like today would be history day. Tomorrow would be mathematics, and that type of thing. And the discipline got out of hand. They just wanted to use us as goats to get those schools that they'd started closed, see. They had started the Charlottesville schools, and had started these schools. They couldn't use the public schools, so then the public schools—really they were oper-ated by the public schools, teachers were being paid. They were using public funds, see. It was quite a bit of confusion, all very interesting.

Well, it wasn't actually what you'd call private. The children didn't have to pay. It was really the city of Charlottesville operating these schools in these places other than the public school building. They gave themselves another name—Charlottesville Educational Association or something like that. Then after February, they said that the black children had not had enough tutoring, so they would be way behind, and they still didn't allow them to go to those schools. And we didn't allow the black children to go back to the black schools. And so, they opened classes up at the school board office with one teacher teaching from the first grade through the senior high school, see. My daughter was senior high school.

They set up classes up at the school board office because we didn't want them to go back to Burley. We would've defeated our purpose if we'd sent them back to a black school. That's what they wanted us to do. See, we would've defeated our purpose if we'd sent them back to a black school.

They had what—the lawyers agreed that they had a legitimate argument, that the black children had not received any education from September to the time the schools were opened. So, they would be behind these whites, and they would lose out in the classroom, see. But they didn't know that we had been tutoring our children. We had some retired teachers and some, well, like my daughter for instance, she had a math teacher and an English teacher that she would go to in the evenings. The regular teachers would come home, and she would go and get the instruction. Same way with the other children. We had a tutoring class up at the Trinity Episcopal Church which was on Tenth and Grady then, for the elementary children.

Black parents of students who were to have been the first to integrate the white high school refused to send their children to the all-black Burley High School; and because black parents were only obeying the law in refusing to send their children to the all-black schools, it became the city's responsibility to provide, in some way, for those black students' education. Consequently, as already mentioned, black students were actually taught at the school board office. Some who graduated during this period of massive resistance received diplomas from no high school in particular but simply from "The City of Charlottesville."

Most respondents agree that the private schools created for white students were actually relocations for the segregated white schools that had been closed. In fact, whites who taught at these specially established educational centers continued to be paid by the city. The inconveniences involved in operating those alternative centers, however, gradually increased to the point where some of the white instructors themselves became clandestinely involved in attempting to persuade the parents of black students to integrate the alternative facilities.

Blacks of course rejected such propositions. Nevertheless, the white-operated alternative centers were closed anyway, due mainly to the difficulty involved in maintaining discipline. Alexander Scott, principal of Burley High School at that time, elaborates further on the rather arduous process.

The few children at first who decided to integrate were taught in the superintendent's office and not in the classroom. This is the first stage. And rather than to open up the schools and carry this out in the beginning stages, there was a short period of time when the students were taught in churches and places, that is, the white schools. The black schools opened. The whites didn't. That was the beginning stage. One or two black students had integrated into the white schools. Very few. They were deal-ing then with the freedom of choice type of thing. Later on, say about 1965, inte-gration had started. So, from 1954 to 1965, there was a process, a gradual process of integration going through several stages.

    I was principal of Burley from 1959 to 1967. These were the last seven or eight years of its existence as a senior high school. And all of the black students came to my school. However, if any students desired to go to the other school by his own freedom or his own choice, nobody stopped him, and he was free to do that. However, we didn't have but a very few students to do that. And as long as you had that extremely lim-ited number of students, there were essentially no problems. Because, by and large, the students they chose were in the higher echelon of the academic potential, and you didn't have trouble there. They fitted in just like the other students did. When they actually began to integrate completely, there were instances of frustration. There weren't problems of any serious nature, but there were frustrations. There were con-ferences to work with teachers, conferences to work with students. However, in far too many instances the transition was not as smooth as it might have been if both sides had really and truly wanted it and really and truly worked for it.

Massive resistance was the plan designed to prevent black students from being educated with whites. Yet by the end of 1959 the Charlottesville public school system had gone through its initial stages of integration. By then a few black students — mostly from the black middle class — had broken through the racial barrier. However, when the greater masses of black students sought to be edu-cated at the previously all-white public schools, racial problems arose once again. Many white teachers became frustrated at having to teach black students whose backgrounds were almost totally alien to theirs. At the same time, black teachers were faced with the prospect of having to prove that they could teach as well as whites. Black and white teachers and students, formerly accustomed to segregation, were suddenly placed in a situation wherein they were forced to interact and directly compete with individuals from a different culture.

    Sherman White, one of the original desegregation suit plaintiffs, praises the NAACP for its efforts during those times; however, like Raymond Bell, he is extremely critical of the recent decline in that organization's "political" effectiveness.

The NAACP was the organization in the city of Charlottesville. And in the '60s it was probably at its best. Late '50s and '60s, it was at its best. But again, blacks started getting some token jobs, and I think the overall feeling was that they felt they had arrived. They didn't need the NAACP anymore. So, they stopped paying their dues. And what had been one of the largest chapters in the whole NAACP through-out the country, with over a thousand members ... in a certain size—category—city or whatever, it was the largest chapter.

    Then it went to 160 members because first of all, people failed to support it, and second of all, the NAACP lost something. It lost a valuable asset that it used to have, and that was to show its concern for its membership. And they did that by simply not being active. They've got so many things built into the present structure of the NAACP, if there's a problem, you've got to do this and you've got to do that. You got to do this and do that before anybody will take any action. They don't react. They don't seem to know how to come to grips with things, like they did back in the other days. And the dedication is not there. The dedication is not there. In other words, Spottswood Robinson, Thurgood Marshall, Sam Tucker dedication is no longer there. The young black coming out of law school now feels like he can work nine to five, make sixty thousand dollars a year, and now they just don't have to.

These people—people like Tucker and Marshall—these fellows paid some very heavy dues. Sometimes they didn't even get paid, you know. And just by the grace of God, the people taking them in and feeding them. And I'm saying that young persons got to experience all that to appreciate it. All I'm saying, though, is they need to have an appreciation of that, and they don't. And it's just like they don't know from where they came. See, if you don't have a past, you can't have a future, you see. And that's our problem. We have no past, or we don't have any memory of the past. And as a result, our future is very bleak.

Another good thing the NAACP did back in the '50s I thought was excellent, and something that really hasn't taken hold in the '80s, hopefully it will, it had a youth chapter, a very active youth chapter. People from New York would come down and see how they were doing, and bring people in. In fact, when I was a school plaintiff, I got a chance to meet someone in Wilmington, Delaware. I still have correspondence with that person in Wilmington, Delaware, that was a plaintiff and successfully got in. They came and related their experiences, what they went through. Well, that was very important. But we had a well-organized youth chapter. We had money.

At one time the premier organization in the struggle for civil rights, the NAACP has since lost much of its luster. From the spectacular careers of chief executives James Weldon Johnson, Walter White, and Roy Wilkins, we have witnessed, in recent years, the dismissal of Director Benjamin Chavis amidst charges of fiscal mismanagement and sexual harassment. From the Legal Defense and Educational Fund's glory days of Charles Hamilton Houston and Thurgood Marshall, we have indeed arrived at a new era where the effectiveness of even that NAACP department is seriously questioned. Sherman White places the blame on a lack of the sort of dedication that existed in earlier years, a dedication that had made people willing to give freely of their time and labor. Those were the days when the NAACP had a clearly defined mission, easier to chart because the general manner of racial discrimination in the United States was such an obvious affront to the most basic human values. On the other hand, in recent years it has become increasingly difficult to determine where and how the battles should be fought and more difficult for would-be financial contributors to feel that support for the organization is still an urgent necessity.

The Political Climate in Charlottesville
before Urban Renewal

Blacks have always had limited political and economic power in both Charlottesville and the surrounding Albemarle County. Particularly during the crucial time when urban renewal was becoming a public issue, blacks had no representation on the city council. Raymond Bell attests that

Not only were there not any neighborhood organizations per se, such as we have today where we have integrated neighborhood associations, but we had no political power. We had no representation on city council. You must remember, at this time, there were no black people elected to city council.

Sherman White reiterates:

There weren't any blacks on the city council. There weren't any blacks in any deci-sion-making position. So, it was very little that they could do to know what was going on, to find out what was going on, because they didn't have anything to do with the power in town, and still have very little.

Charlottesville's overall population in 1960 was 29,427.[6] Blacks made up about 19 percent of that number and had a voter registration of 1300.[7] The city was by this time near the end of its evolution "from a large country town into a small metropolitan center."[8] Yet while the white population had grown — 57 percent from 1930 to 1962 — with the increase in business and industrializa-tion, the number of blacks living there during those same decades remained virtually unchanged.[9]

Although many black citizens who got the opportunity to leave Char-lottesville never returned to live in their hometown, other blacks enjoyed Char-lottesville's small-town atmosphere and had no desire to leave. Mattie Thompkins, for example, explains why she never left.

Virginia is about the best place anybody can live, because I've lived here all my life, and I've been to visit several cities like D.C., Philadelphia. I do not like it.

This is Charlottesville, Virginia. I don't know about the other parts. There are the other parts of Virginia. I mean exactly Charlottesville, because I've lived here, and like I say, I'll go anywhere else to visit, but not to stay.

Seems like to me you have more freedom. You don't have to be at home and be afraid, because like I said, when you live in the city, when you've got these bars on the door, these double padlocks—about five, six, or seven locks on one door—and then you've got to worry about going to sleep at night, whether somebody is going to come in here and kill you. I don't feel that's safe at all. I can shut these doors here and go in there and go to bed. I ain't got to worry about nobody coming in here. And I say this because, you know, I don't need to live in fear. It's not necessary. And I feel that is nothing but fear when you live in the city.

Raymond Bell and George Ferguson had expressed regret over the exodus of some blacks from Charlottesville; however, Thompkins presents us with a different perspective that in recent years has not been all that unusual as the North has ceased to be the "promised land" that it was thought of in earlier years. Now the migration has reversed itself, and blacks are returning to live in the South, that same South from which earlier generations of blacks fled in desperation.

Yet the fact remains that in the 1960s, blacks had little access to political power in Charlottesville. As Sadie Mason states,

We were in the minority. We had no vote here, no say-so. I had no say-so because my vote didn't mean anything. So, I got to the point, I was like voting for anything because I knew I wouldn't change anything. Now, you can quote me on that. Why vote when you know you're outnumbered? I'm just going to tell it to you like it is. I'm glad to speak my piece for a change. My husband would probably tell me don't talk too much, but I don't like it.

Others nonetheless hold a different view, such as Laura Franklin, who recalls the influence of Nannie Cox Jackson.

I voted when I joined the Eastern Star. And Mrs. Jackson said she wanted every person in the Eastern Star to vote.

Thomas Inge was persuaded in a similar fashion.

My father always said that no one 21 could live in this house unless they went and voted, registered to vote. That's how strong he advocated voting. He said you weren't a real citizen if you didn't vote, if you didn't take advantage of it.

George Ferguson, on the other hand, agrees with Sadie Mason.

We voted, but that didn't carry a whole lot of weight—city and state. They voted for everything that you could vote for. But just like it is now—maybe the percentage is higher now than it was then—but we still don't have enough black votes.

Indeed when four white men — three Democrats and one Republican — ran for the three vacant city council seats in 1960, they did not have much to worry about from the pool of potential black voters. As we mentioned earlier, Charles Johnson, a black funeral director, was defeated at the Democratic primary stage.

S. Dexter Forbes, one of the Democratic nominees, urged city residents to vote against public housing. The following is a report printed by the *Daily Progress* on a speech prepared by Forbes for radio broadcast:

> S. Dexter Forbes, Democratic candidate for election to City Council in tomorrow's balloting, says in a speech prepared for radio delivery today that he urges the city's residents to vote against public housing in tomorrow's referendum.
>
> The other two Democratic candidates in tomorrow's election — Bernard J. Haggerty and Lindsay B. Mount — have scheduled radio speeches today urging voters to support redevelopment and public housing.

R. E. Lee, lone Republican candidate, is also a supporter of the redevelopment and housing program. The four candidates are running for three seats subject to tomorrow's election.

"You can provide new buildings for people to live in, but can't provide new habits or morals for those people," Forbes says. "When federal money is accepted by a municipality for such projects, it is a clear indication that they are not willing to undertake it themselves, and it is also a clear source of encouragement to our representatives in Washington to make further appropriations for such projects."

Forbes says that everyone would like to have "our so-called slum areas cleaned up and the people living in these areas rehabilitated," but that he is not in accord with the method proposed by the Charlottesville Redevelopment and Housing Authority.

"These slums, so-called, did not happen overnight," Forbes says. "Nor did they come last year or the year before. They have been with us a long, long time, and I can see no justification for trying to clean them up in one clear swoop.

"Let it be done with our own money and gradually with the hope that many of the dwellings can be remodeled and made to conform to the present City Code. I feel certain that a method can be found to improve the Vinegar Hill area without using federal money and we will be proud of our accomplishment. I urge you to vote against public housing."[10]

Though he argued against the proposed urban renewal plan, one wonders what motivated him to take this position. He made an important point as he stressed that poor housing conditions "did not happen overnight." And his suggestion that certain of the existing dwellings be remodeled and brought up to an acceptable standard seemed on one hand to be a position that had the best interests of Vinegar Hill residents in mind. But as one reads Forbes's statement more closely, what becomes clear is that he was primarily concerned about the prospect that Charlottesville would get more and more enmeshed in the intricate process of providing lower-income housing and more and more dependent on the federal government to support those housing ventures.

Closer analysis also reveals that Forbes spoke not so much about rehabilitating the buildings as of rehabilitating "the people living in these areas." Keep in mind that right there on the Hill were black entrepreneurs of practically every sort. Black educators lived there as well. There were churches and the Jefferson School. The very fact that such a community had developed so fully during the latter part of the nineteenth century, and on into a significant portion of the twentieth century, is nothing short of phenomenal. It was an absolute insult that anyone would dare say that such extraordinary people, the individuals themselves, needed to be rehabilitated.

Perhaps when Forbes declared that "you ... can't provide new habits or morals for those people," he had specific reference to the lower classes of blacks who lived on the Hill. But many of "those people" were the grandchildren of slaves who understood quite well what they had to do to survive in a society that had shut them out and isolated them, in the first place, in one general section of Charlottesville.

Aerial view of Vinegar Hill in the early 1960s before renewal.

Even as late as the 1960s, a quasi slavery still existed. Many Vinegar Hill residents, such as Connie Brooks and Drusilla Hutchinson, were maids and cooks. They were janitors like Mattie Thompkins's father and washerwomen such as those to whom Laura Franklin refers. From various locations in and around the University of Virginia to the outlying country clubs, they were there to do the cooking and cleaning, sometimes walking miles in the dark to get to their places of employment. Far from needing any "new habits or morals," those former residents were patiently laying the groundwork for later generations of African Americans to build upon.

But Forbes could not have understood all that. Nor could the other white candidates, because the black and white cultures in Charlottesville had been kept so rigidly divided. As far as the price Forbes paid for his ignorance, he wound up losing the election by 45 votes to R. E. Lee, a Republican who supported the urban renewal project.

Included on that ballot was the Vinegar Hill referendum. It allowed voters to answer either affirmatively or negatively regarding two related issues:

1) the continuation of the powers of the Redevelopment and Housing Authority
2) the redevelopment of Vinegar Hill and location of public housing near the intersection of Hartman's Mill Road and Ridge Street

The first question, involving a grant of life to the previously dormant Redevelopment and Housing Authority, was answered affirmatively by a margin of 206 votes.[11] The issue of whether that authority should proceed with its plans to redevelop the particular area of Vinegar Hill was decided affirmatively by an even closer margin — 23 votes.[12]

With such narrow margins of victory in the election, as well as the referendum, one wonders whom urban renewal was most designed to accommodate. Charles Johnson, who was unable to get the nomination from his party, gives this perspective on housing conditions:

Every home in the area was substandard that they tore up. Some I don't think you could even call homes really. They were just equivalent to slave shacks.

That was his view of Vinegar Hill. Of the place to which Hill residents were to be moved, the former city council aspirant contends that

Cox's Row was just some slave-type shanties put up by some unscrupulous whites. It was just something to put blacks in, but they really had no comfort.

So, the location for the new housing project was set at a place called Cox's Row, a location that was actually just blocks away from the Hill itself. But it was far enough away from the downtown business district to give central Charlottesville a whole new cultural flavor.

Though rapidly expanding, a major goal of the powers-that-be in Charlottesville was to retain as much of the small-town atmosphere that made it an attractive place to live for a variety of people. So, in some respects it is inappropriate to compare what took place on the Hill to processes of gentrification that have been occurring recently in larger cities across the nation. In places like New York City, for example, droves of people who might easily have been suburbanites are moving into inner-city locations that were once almost entirely the domain of working-class families and the temporarily or permanently unemployed. New York public-policy maker Peter Marcuse describes the phenomenon:

> This process has two aspects: the shift from manufacturing to services, from reliance on mid-level skills to automation and de-skilling, on the one hand, which renders redundant large parts of the workforce and reduces lower-income rent-paying ability; and the increasing professionalization and concentration of management and technical functions, on the other, which creates additional higher-income demand for housing. These processes have spatial consequences: blue-collar workers are no longer needed in such numbers downtown; professional and technical workers are in ever-increasing demand there.... For the gentrifiers, all roads lead to downtown. For the poor, all roads lead to abandonment.[13]

Charlottesville never became a center for manufacturing, but the blue-collar workers to whom Marcuse refers, the ones that he contends are no longer needed, might easily be compared to former Vinegar Hill residents who were deemed ripe for removal by the city. They were expendable and indeed as the city advanced in terms of modernization and prestige, many African Americans who had been living on the Hill all of their lives were faced with the prospect that their own neighborhood would no longer sustain even their humble lifestyles. In places like New York, working-class poor and the unemployed were forced to abandon the places they had rented because prices escalated during the years of gentrification, whereas in Charlottesville, the relocation of blacks occurred in one fell swoop as the Hill was first summarily demolished and then slowly rebuilt in only incremental stages that left little opportunity for the previous black residents to return.

The gentrification phenomenon has indeed occurred to some extent in inner-city Charlottesville. Downtown has redeveloped into an exceedingly attractive place for certain types of businesses and individuals who are fortunate enough to have the necessary financial wherewithal. But even more intriguing than the feature of gentrification is the manner in which urban renewal has contributed to making the city of Charlottesville an extraordinary drawing card, attracting celebrities from every walk of life — from the expected academics such as Rita Dove, Richard Rorty, and Nathan Scott to other famous writers such as Rita Mae Brown, Mary Lee Settle, and John Grisham; from television broadcasters Katie Couric and Howie Long to actors and actresses whose ranks in the surrounding countryside now include Tim and Daphne Reid and Kate Jackson. In fact, most of the celebrities do not live in Charlottesville outright but on the outskirts of town, taking in the local culture from time to time even as they maintain their privacy. It is a lifestyle that many would envy, a lifestyle that, at any rate, must certainly be pondered in light of the city's racial past, contemporary racial circumstances, and the deceptive characterization of Charlottesville as the epitome of quaintness.

CHAPTER FOUR

RELOCATION

Westhaven

By 1949 the United States Congress had come to the conclusion that the 1937 Urban Renewal Act was too limited, so it enacted further provisions outlining how renewal could be effected in a wider variety of instances. Then in 1954 even more provisions were enacted so that renewal implementation could be accomplished with a simpler methodology. That same year, the Supreme Court rendered its *Berman v. Parker* decision, giving legal sanction to the clearance of entire neighborhoods and providing the rationale for what was to become three decades of effort to improve America's inner cities.[1] In ruling on a renewal plan to be undertaken in Washington, D.C., the Court rendered this explanation:

> The experts concluded that if the community were to be healthy, if it were not to revert again to a blighted or slum area, as though possessed of a congenital disease, the area must be planned as a whole. It was not enough, they believed, to remove existing buildings that were unsanitary or unsightly. It was important to redesign the whole area so as to eliminate the conditions that cause slums — the overcrowding of dwellings, the lack of parks, the lack of adequate streets and alleys, the absence of recreational areas, the lack of light and air, the presence of outmoded street patterns. It was believed that the piecemeal approach, the removal of individual structures that were offensive, would be only a palliative. The entire area needed redesigning so that a balanced, integrated plan could be developed for the region, including not only new homes but also schools, churches, parks, streets and shopping centers.[2]

It is useful to consider that Gene Arrington, who was the Charlottesville Redevelopment and Housing Authority director at the time of renewal, described Vinegar Hill in terms strikingly similar to how Charles Johnson viewed the area and how the Supreme Court in *Berman* viewed the proposed renewal site in Washington.

Concerning Vinegar Hill, Arrington declares, "Everyone wanted to stay in 1960."[3] He remembers, in fact, being hated by many who simply wanted to stay where they were. Nevertheless, he insists that the renewal project as it was conducted was designed to be most beneficial to those who would be displaced:

I still believe it was the only way to help that neighborhood. How else were you going to do it? I'm convinced. We took those people out of the slums. Even in Westhaven, we gave them the best housing they ever had. Now people say, "But people were uprooted." No question about it, we moved people out. People had roots there, and that's the sad part of it.

I was the most unpopular man in the community, at least the black community. When you sit in a living room and that woman says to you, "Mr. Arrington," with tears running down her face, "if you just let me die here; I've lived here all my life; I've only got a few years left," of course you feel sympathy for them. But you do what you have to do, what's good for the community. And I think what we did was for the good of the community.

That woman moved up Preston Avenue into a nice brick house. She wasn't made whole, but we helped her out. She had means. We never had any planning in the beginning. Things were plopped down, and that was that. The decay of the core cities couldn't be arrested. The idea was to start over.

I visited those row houses. I remember one place. It was so dark inside, you couldn't see. You walked in the kitchen, and there was another room, and a two-by-four right inside the door. I hit my head. I couldn't see, it was so dark. I thought someone had hit me. The woman, a real nice lady, said, "Oh, Mr. Arrington, I put that board there to hold up that cardboard on the ceiling so the rain will run off and not leak on the bed." You'd see curtains, a Bible. I saw a lot of home pride, the best that they could.

The commercial buildings leaned side by side, and that was all that held them up. You could go underneath those buildings and take your fingernail and scrape the mortar.

People have their own opinion—"Hell no! It isn't worth it! You're uprooting people." But here's a choice success story: A man who was paying forty dollars a month, a hardworking guy who strived to be a homeowner but didn't have the down payment— maybe he had three hundred dollars in the bank— he bought himself a house on Azalea Drive, and we gave him an additional four thousand dollars. We gave him the down payment. We saw he could carry it. Some people don't want to pay rent. They have jobs and all, but they don't want to pay any rent. They don't care where they live. And I don't think everyone should be a homeowner. I don't. There are some people who just can't carry it. We asked them, "Where do you work? How many people in your family? How much money do you have in the bank?" If they were eligible for two thousand dollars matching funds, they got four thousand dollars. Tenants become homeowners. That's beautiful.

When I moved them in, all of a sudden the clothes, when they washed them, I noticed were whiter. And I asked my wife, and she said it was the warm water. Hot water brightens up clothes. I visited over there, and the two things they always mentioned, "Oh, Mr. Arrington, all that wonderful heat, and all that nice warm water." They were the rewards I got. I had a part in that.[4]

The planning for the removal of Vinegar Hill residents to a nearby project site had begun by 1958. It took approximately two years, however, for the *public* presentation of a plan. Once the 1960 referendum for renewal on the Hill was passed, it took an additional two years to locate a definite removal site for residents who would otherwise be without housing. With the power vested by Title 36 of the Code of Virginia, the Charlottesville Redevelopment and Housing Authority leveled Vinegar Hill, leaving in its wake the absolute ruins of what had once been the hub of Charlottesville black society.

The housing authority lists 158 families as having been residents of Vinegar Hill just before urban removal took place. Eighteen of those families were white. Of all the families located on the Hill, 22 were homeowners and 136 were tenants. Those who were homeowners received the fair market value for their property. Their moving expenses were also covered by the city. Moreover, allotments were assigned for down payments in cases where former homeowners on the Hill had arranged for the purchase of a new home.

Tenants from both Cox's Row, the site for relocation, and Vinegar Hill were encouraged to move into the specially constructed, 225-unit Westhaven Public Housing Project. One hundred thirty-two Vinegar Hill tenants were declared financially eligible for welfare benefits and public housing.[5] Consequently, the overwhelming majority of that group accepted the move to Hardy Drive, which was the major street where the housing project was located.

Hardy Drive is named after the late Reverend Royal Brown Hardy who, from 1892 to 1917, pastored Mount Zion Baptist Church, one of two churches that had to be relocated due to urban renewal. Born in Botetourt County, near Roanoke, Virginia, he later attended the Richmond Theological Seminary and upon arriving in Charlottesville became an ardent social reformer who was especially noted for leading the fight to close barrooms.

The project name "Westhaven" was a dedication by the housing authority to the deceased black barber, John West. West, who was born a slave, moved to Charlottesville as the adopted son of Nancy West, a freedwoman who worked as a milliner. Legend has it that when John West was a boy, he saved the life of Confederate cavalry leader John Mosby by warning him that Union soldiers were secretly approaching. Galloping out of town, the grateful Mosby tossed a silver dollar to the youngster.

That silver dollar was an omen of good things to come, for West eventually amassed a fortune in real estate holdings, including property in Albemarle and Fluvanna counties, and 700 acres in the Blue Ridge Mountains. He had been one of the "gentlemen barbers" who managed to generate a lucrative business, cutting white men's hair. Even barbershops were segregated in those days; however, black barbers could also maintain an establishment that catered solely to white customers. As a child living on Vinegar Hill, George Ferguson was in a good position to observe firsthand those intriguing circumstances of the barbering trade:

When I was a child, there was only one barbershop run by whites, by a white man that was for whites. The rest of the barbershops were run by blacks that served whites. And we had several beautiful barbershops here that were owned by blacks, and they catered to the whites. And, of course, you know the segregation and so forth. And evidently it must have been a very lucrative business because we have several families here that owned real estate, not only homes they lived in, but other real estate. They educated their children. At that time, we had to pay, or our parents had to pay for us to go to high school. Parents would send us away to high school, and it had to be paid for.

In particular, Ferguson recalls the West legacy:

Mr. West's property ran all the way back to Commerce Street. He was a barber. They called him a gentleman's barber, but he was a gentleman himself. He had a very large family. He owned quite a bit of real estate in Charlottesville, and he was one of the few black men to die worth over a quarter of a million dollars, as they reported.

John West. And they named Westhaven after him. I'm almost certain that West Street was named for Mr. West. He owned the property which is now occupied by the Monticello Dairy. In other words, that property ran from West Street over to Preston Avenue, very big field there. He owned that land, and it was later sold to the owners of Monticello Dairy. Grady Avenue stopped at Tenth Street at that time. Then after Monticello Dairy bought it, that street came through.

Mr. West also owned, going further down Main Street, two or three buildings there. I can remember in one of the buildings there was a printing office that was owned by Mr. John Shelton and a Mr. Barber. I can't think of Mr. Barber's name now—first name. They had this printing office, and they put out a little newspaper called "The Messenger."

Laura Franklin confirms the fact that of all the names submitted for consideration, Hardy and West were the ones finally selected for the purposes of dedicating the housing project and its major thoroughfare.

Yeah, Hardy Drive. That's named after Mr. Hardy. And Westhaven is named after Mr. West, the man that was on Main Street, I told you, that had the house that was farm-like. And a preacher here that was a pastor at Mount Zion Church for a number of years, that's who Hardy Drive is named after, a preacher.

Booker Reaves also remembers:

Westhaven was built, and, of course, Hardy Drive—that's the name of the street through there—that was named for a minister who used to be a Reverend Hardy at Mount Zion Baptist Church on Ridge Street. He and his family lived on Dice Street. And then, of course, Westhaven was named for Mr. West, who was a pretty well-to-do black man who lived on Main Street in the area where Russell Mooney used to be, down in that area. The big house they lived in on Main Street. He ran a barbershop for whites. And he accumulated quite a lot of wealth. And so, when they were naming Hardy Drive, they just named the whole area Westhaven in honor of this Mr. West.

In naming Hardy Drive and Westhaven, the city took advantage of the opportunity to commemorate two of the most prominent black citizens ever to have lived in the Vinegar Hill area.

But what about the masses of former Hill residents? Were their lives, as Gene Arrington asserts, really made sufficiently better? In their essay "Legal and Governmental Issues in Urban Renewal," social scientists Wilton Sogg and Warren Wertheimer offer this advice: "In the relocation of individuals and families displaced from a renewal area, it is crucial that the ultimate objectives of urban renewal be considered. These persons must be relocated in such a way as to prevent the areas to which they move from becoming new slums. Their relocation must be supervised in order to act as an affirmative force in controlling the future development of the city."[6] Sogg and Wertheimer specify that the "ultimate objectives" of an urban renewal program must include special consideration for the new environment of those who are about to be relocated. The authors urge that there be a strong governmental concern for citizens who are subjected to removal. But they also stress "future development of the city" as an important concern. Paradoxically enough, though, in presenting these considerations they have also exposed a potential conflict, for what is beneficial for the city and what is beneficial to people subject to relocation might very well be two different things.

Quite a few respondents feel that the move away from Vinegar Hill was beneficial. Reaves, who first taught at and then became the principal of the Jefferson School, renders the following assessment:

Although some people may not have liked it at the time, I think it was good because most people, most people who moved out of Vinegar Hill, as far as I can see, have better economic conditions than they had in Vinegar Hill, and they probably loved what they had in Vinegar Hill. They liked the idea of two rooms and maybe a wood stove in the kitchen and that sort of thing. But now they have been able to move out and share some of the things that other people in this world are sharing, rather than have to live just like people did in slavery times. That's the way I feel about it.

I'll tell you, the houses down there weren't the kind that you could remodel. They were just, well, I guess in the whole section there wasn't—well, first of all, let me say this. They weren't using cinderblocks hardly at all before World War II, and the houses were old wooden houses that had rotted out and rotted the foundation. None of them had very strong foundations, and I thought that most of them didn't, so therefore there weren't things that you'd want to remodel. So, it's best they got torn out and then started all over again.

Thomas Inge, in general, supports that conclusion.

I think the black people had gained a lot from urban renewal. One thing that people who went over to Westhaven were, some of them had no modern conveniences at all—outside privies and that sort of thing, and outside falseproof toilets—some of them, and that was quite a step up, I think, as far as living conditions were concerned. But some people don't like to be in those things. They want to be out where they feel free. They don't want to be inseparable, but I think they lived there and learned to like it. I don't know whether you ever visited any of those apartments, but they're very, very nice.

In spite of his support for the housing project, Inge still has certain reservations that have to do with a congested living style as compared to what had been, on the Hill, a largely rural setting.

Alexander Scott also approves of the Westhaven housing project, though with some qualification:

The housing at Westhaven, per se, I don't think was anything wrong with it when it was built. Nor has it been too badly kept. I think the people have kept it pretty well. I'm sure the long arm of the law has laid down some good, strong advisory regulations to cause this. Yes, when it first was built, the homes were nice. They built very nice homes. They were well-constructed.

However, I realize that this may have to be an intermediary step for people to be housed. Philosophically, my opinion is that every man and every family should own a certain portion of this soil, of this dirt, and of these homes. And I think this should be the aspiration of the family. But I realize that some intermediary step will have to be taken because many people cannot proceed to purchase. There may be a time when they will have to do what they're doing now, and this is to rent and to rent, and if they have to rent, it's always best for them to live in decent homes. I don't look at this as the ultimate.

I think any family with enough get-up-and-go and with enough income to pay the rent that is charged in the city of Charlottesville, with proper knowledge of budgeting, can purchase his own home if he chooses to do so. Philosophically, I would like to see people purchase their own homes because I think they have a great deal more interest in what is there. But I'm sure the intermediary step will have to be taken in practically every core city because you have numbers of persons who can't get that 10 percent down payment. They aren't veterans. They haven't saved two thousand or five thousand. The economy is so that they probably can't. They might even have two or three children. You know, milk and butter has to come before homes.

There is something of a contradiction in Scott's analysis because even as he champions the goal of home ownership as a prospect for former Vinegar Hill residents, he credits law enforcement agents for having forced Westhaven to maintain its livable condition. Though there have been many people in America who have been able to pull themselves up by their bootstraps even out of deplorable conditions, it is unlikely that an inner-city housing project could, for the general population, satisfy the "intermediary step" proposition of Scott's theoretical design.

In analyzing the implementation of public housing programs throughout the nation, sociologist Chester Hartman observes, "It is an inescapable conclusion that relocation has been only an ancillary component of the renewal process; were this not the case, the community would find totally unacceptable 'slum clearance' projects which leave as many as two-thirds of the displaced families still living in substandard conditions, or which actually increase the incidence of overcrowding."[7] Hartman, in distinguishing between renewal and relocation, expresses the inappropriateness of municipalities giving a lower priority to the latter. Was the city of Charlottesville guilty of that indiscretion?

Enola Ford, who worked as a beautician and as a housekeeper, remains ambivalent about the plan that called for the vast majority of Vinegar Hill residents to move into Westhaven.

I guess it was better all the way around because some of those places down there were terrible. But then it's getting the same up there in the projects, because most of them are up there in the projects.

Rebecca McGinness also has difficulty assessing whether the move to Westhaven was mostly bad or good.

In some instances it has been good come out of it. And in other instances it's not. Some of these people, who had good homes that they had lived in for years, felt very uneasy about it. And then the urban renewal put all the people together, all kinds of people together. And that made it kinda congesting-like. And they didn't get along, so I understand, so well. Too much, you know, too much togetherness.

A major purpose of any urban renewal program should be to help city residents who have suffered in the past from substandard living conditions, but former Harvard Law School professor Derrick Bell reiterates Hartman's view that, in actuality, such residents are often not the city's primary concern:

> Slum clearance has not been for the benefit of slum residents, nor has slum rehabilitation benefited families of low and modest incomes. Instead, cities have substituted their own goals for national housing goals because solving the housing problem of the poor does not help solve the cities' financial problems; does not improve the tax rate; does not improve the cities' competitive position vis-a-vis the suburbs; and does not gain national recognition for leadership in creating symbols of civic grandeur.
>
> Urban renewal has eliminated pockets of dilapidated housing and blight in core cities and suburbs, reaped windfall profits for real estate investors, and paved the way for new public monuments. But urban renewal has hurt and scattered the poor and Negroes, while subsidizing the right of the more affluent to replace them, as the "highest and best use of the land." Except in private, the federal government refuses to admit this fact: slum clearance has failed to provide decent housing for slum-dwellers. Urban renewal and public housing programs have intensified segregation of Negroes in inner city ghettos.[8]

Bell argues that urban renewal has failed to improve the predicament of poor, inner-city blacks. Instead, such programs have created new slum environments and have basically left blacks in the same situation that they were in before such housing programs were begun.

Mattie Thompkins recalls that her family was the second one to move into Westhaven. At first she and other family members were excited, but then a sad phenomenon became all too apparent.

After they moved, they didn't have to worry about no coal stove, cutting wood, or nothing else—leaking ceilings or nothing. They were just, seems like to me, in luxury because of the fact everything was modern. And it was nice. At one time, seems like Hardy Drive, when we moved in, was real nice.

And then after a certain amount of years, anybody live in one place, you know, it gets to be rowdy and everything. At one time it was strictly people coming in with families and everything. But then after a while, they had these young people coming in on welfare with the babies and this and that, you know, and it got to be nothing but like a ghetto. If it wasn't for my mother living up in there, they wouldn't even see me in Hardy Drive. Because they just don't want to do nothing but lay around.

If they would just get up off of that stuff and do something and make something of themselves instead of laying there and just doing nothing, you know, just don't care. "Well, we're getting our living money. We work every month, we're getting our money." You know, like they done gone out here and got a job somewhere. They know they can get this. The government is giving it to them because they say you can go out here and have one child, you can get on welfare, you can get a place to live. They know that.

Like so many others, Thompkins portrays Westhaven as having been a respectable community in its initial years. But as time passed, others, in addition to former Hill residents, qualified for some type of public assistance and were allowed to move into the project. Whether the Westhaven residents themselves were to blame for the decline, or the city of Charlottesville for helping to perpetuate what we now know as a cycle of dependency, the incontrovertible fact remains that the dilemma in general has become one of our most pressing social concerns.

Many Americans will argue that the use of welfare provisions, as a be-all-that-ends-all for the underprivileged classes, caused this cycle of dependency. Sherman White, for example, blames the Democratic Party:

I personally just feel that the Democrats had these social programs as an opiate to blacks and minorities, and get you caught up on food stamps, get you hung up on this and that so you become less dependent on yourself. So, now we got family after family after family on welfare, generation after generation. Hence, you never have a chance to stand on your own feet.

Although we as a society have argued back and forth about whether or not blacks should be able in substantial numbers to remove themselves from the welfare rolls, it is useful to consider what Andrew Billingsley and Jeanne Giovannoni say in their book *Children of the Storm*. Commenting on the tendency to blame those who have been socially disadvantaged, the authors contend, "This phenomenon is, of course, not unique to child welfare; most social institutions in this country, failing as they have to overcome the racism that is so much a part of them, also have their supporting mythologies which ultimately place the blame for the failure on Black people."[9] Some, like Mattie Thompkins, were able to overcome the racism of the 1950s and 1960s. They built on the sacrifice of their parents and managed to become self-sufficient.

But the Reverend Elisha Hall tells of another type of individual, the person who does not fare as well against the taunts and jeers of an increasingly materialistic and accusing world. According to this pastor, the Westhaven residents have suffered from more than just poverty.

They were affected educationally, and they're still suffering from that stigma. In the high schools, when the students find out that you're from Hardy Drive, you're looked down upon—"You're from Hardy Drive." You go to get a job, you from Hardy Drive, the man—the employer has a tendency to be a little slow to hire you. Even in the church, you find even some of the blacks saying, "You know, this person is from Hardy Drive?" So, it still carries that stigma. It has affected them educationally, economically, and socially. They have been affected. And it's very unfortunate. And many of them, as I said, are suffering from that stigma now.

The End of an Era

Life on Vinegar Hill had been a somewhat different situation. When the Hill existed as a black neighborhood, it was a community composed variously of those who were wealthy, middle class, and poor. Hall acknowledges the prior diversity:

Some of the houses on Vinegar Hill were very, very good standard houses. Some of them weren't. They were infested with rats. The houses—the owners violated every code in the book as far as how they looked. And the upkeep—some of them were beyond repair.

Thomas Johnson declares that

It was really strange because like right behind the stores that they had there, you know, there were a lot of slum houses in that particular area. Just on the other side of the street, you had some really nice houses from one end of the block to the other end.

Speaking again from the dual perspective of having first been a student and then a principal at the Jefferson School, Booker Reaves offers these insights:

When I was a student there in the '30s, I lived on Ridge Street behind the railroad. Anyway, there was a Vinegar Hill area that had, as I recall, four main streets

One of the nicer homes on Vinegar Hill before renewal.

through it. There was Commerce Street, I guess you heard that name, Williams Street, Page Street, Third Street, and Irvin Street. Those four were the main ones. Now, some of those streets had some of the homes of the better class of Charlottesville black people, at that time, and they were well-kept homes. And they were people who had good jobs. And some of them were hairdressers. Some of them were barbers who were downtown.

And then there was a church, two churches in the Vinegar Hill section. One of them is still in existence, but it's the Zion Union here on Preston Avenue. It moved from Vinegar Hill and built a new church. And the other one was Shiloh Baptist Church, and that was a very nice church. That was on Commerce Street as you're going down from, well, you can't go down, but where King's is now.

And there were some very nice homes down there. Of course, there were some that were in need of repair. But in spite of all that, the people who lived down there—the sort of well-to-do and the ones who did not have much income and sort of lived from hand to mouth—had a good relationship as far as the school went. Because all of those children came to Jefferson School. And as far as conflicts go between the children from that area coming to Jefferson School, I had no problems with that at all, as principal.

And the teachers would say the same thing. As a matter of fact, I could name

Zion Union Baptist Church, rebuilt off of Vinegar Hill after urban renewal.

you teachers who have worked in the Charlottesville school system who were born and bred down there and grew up and worked in Charlottesville and Albemarle County. And because they were kinds of families who were strugglers, they worked and had their kids in college. So, Vinegar Hill wasn't all bad when I came along.

I was in school and finished high school in the middle '30s. And Vinegar Hill was probably something that happened in the '80s, back right after the Civil War....

Shiloh Baptist Church, well it was beginning to decline in the early, I'd say, in the '30s. And then, of course, Zion Union had a very strong minister, Reverend Kennedy. He has children living here in Charlottesville now. Ethel Kennedy and Ike Kennedy and Mrs.—the lady who used to run the kindergarten here on Anderson Street. And Reverend Kennedy lived out in the county, out in Earlysville.

Any animosity that might have existed between the black social classes appears to have been minimal because they all were involved, to some degree or another, in the process of racial uplift. Especially before and during the push for integration, community commitment was essential.

The churches that had existed on Vinegar Hill were an essential source of unity for that black community. Shiloh Baptist Church had the smaller congregation of the two churches that were forced to relocate. Already in a state of decline, it was further disadvantaged by having to move. On the other hand, Zion Union Baptist Church had a larger constituency and was able to flourish even after urban renewal forced its move to a new location. Laura Franklin recalls

Zion Union. That was right down on Fourth Street, a little bit from us, across over from the school. And they had to move. That's why they had to build a new church.

Raymond Bell confirms this:

Zion Union was on Fourth Street and in Vinegar Hill. And that was, of course, torn down, and they moved up to Preston Avenue. That church was one of the black churches that became a victim of that renewal. Zion Union. Of course, they paid for the church and they built another one.

Understanding the potential for even more serious repercussions than what would occur with regard to residential and business life, the city sought especially to lessen the impact of renewal on religious institutions.

In further listening to the various respondents, one gets a sense of just how important those churches had been. Thomas Inge says that

Most of the leisure time was spent in church activities, I suppose, because when I was a youngster, the church was as much a social center as it was a religious center.

Drusilla Hutchinson views the church as having been a means whereby she could keep her children out of trouble.

I went to church when I wasn't working. But I was working, and I couldn't go to church. I was working on Sundays, but our children went.

Rebecca McGinness is also enlightening with regard to the church's role in the Hill community.

Everything practically that Negroes had centered around the church because they didn't have any other place to go. So, they belonged to the church. It played an important role in the lives of the people. The ministers in the community, I think they've done more for the black people than anybody else.

However, Sherman White has a different opinion:

I, for one, am overall disappointed with churches, black churches in the community, because I don't think they have done enough in this regard. We have five or six different churches. It would seem to me that it would be smart if the churches would come together and combine their resources instead of going off in all these multitude of directions to protect their little empire. They could come together and set the tone. They could, into themselves, use their funds and resources to help blacks get started in business, give them low interest loans, help finance, be the backers of blacks going into business for themselves.

I really think the church, the black church for one, is just—In the County of Albemarle, I betcha we got 80 little churches. Why do we need all of them? I mean, why don't they combine their resources and have one or two major churches and use those resources to help, in turn, their members rather than seeing ministers—and I tell you the ministers are guilty. A lot of ministers are guilty of just feathering their own nest. "To heck with the congregation. What can I get out of it? Are they gonna pay my house note? Are they gonna pay my utility bill?" That's all they care about. They don't care about the salvation or the sufferings or the improvement or prosperity of their members. They're just concerned about their own prosperity.

White's point is well taken, for there have always been black ministers, and ministers in general, who are more concerned with making money than with saving souls. It is useful in that vein to consider what sociologist E. Franklin Frazier expressed in his treatise, *The Negro Church in America*:

> Let us not forget, however, the control exercised by the Negro was exercised by dominating personalities. Frequently, they were the preachers who had become leaders of Negroes because of their talents and ability to govern men. In the Baptist Churches in which the majority of the Negroes have always been concentrated there was even greater opportunity for self-assertion and the assumption of leadership on the part of strong men. This naturally resulted in a pattern of autocratic leadership which has spilled over into most aspects of organized social life among Negroes, especially in as much as many forms of organized social life have grown out of the church and have come under the dominant leadership of Negro preachers.[10]

As far back as slavery, there have been personalities who amassed their leadership skills and power through the avenue of the black church. Yet as problematic as that process might indeed be, it cannot be denied that such leaders were at the forefront of the efforts for black advancement. Such was the significance of churches on the Hill that were a vital source for the fulfillment of numerous community needs.

And there were other key organizations that contributed to life on the Hill. Laura Franklin attests that

When my husband and I, when we went out, we went to a lot of parties because they had a lot of clubs in Charlottesville, and they still do. And my aunt was in a Secret Twelve Club. And at Christmas time, we just went to parties every night because they would invite another club, and they'd be going all that time. And then they'd meet at people's homes once a month, and I think they enjoyed that, serving meals.

Franklin continues:

I think the Eastern Star is a good organization, and they helped with the nursery out on Ridge Street. And as I said, they gave the money for polio. The money, they sent to Alabama for polio. And then if people needed help sometime, they'd write letters to them, and they often gave a donation.

And then I belonged to a club called Phillis Wheatley, and that's named after a colored lady. That's a federated club, instead of regular club. We had four or five clubs, federated clubs. That was a club that started to help girls. We were girls. But now that's not operating by themselves. I think white people are in with that now.

Secret Twelve. That's also where my husband was a member, and they did some good work, helping people when they needed it, and things.

Such organizations have a long and distinguished history. Eminent historian John Hope Franklin has expounded on what the circumstances were surrounding their development:

> Free Negroes held their fraternal organizations and benevolent societies in high esteem. The Masons continued to flourish during the generation immediately preceding the Civil War. In Maryland, for example, they had grown to the point by 1845 where it became desirable to form the First Colored Grand Lodge, and two years later another was set up. In 1843, under the leadership of Peter Ogden, a group of free Negroes organized the Grand United Order of Odd Fellows, which became one of the major Negro fraternal organizations. Negroes found it desirable to bind themselves together for social and cultural uplift, economic advancement, and mutual relief. Thus, a large number of benevolent societies sprang into existence, some of which were secret.[11]

Franklin further informs us that "secret orders — the International Order of Good Samaritans, the Ancient Sons of Israel, the Grand United Order of True Reformers, and the Independent Order of St. Luke — offered insurance against sickness and death, aided widows and orphans of deceased members, and gave opportunities for social intercourse."[12] Organizations similar to those functioned quite effectively on the Hill, rendering (as did the churches) services that private individuals and local government could not or would not provide. With considerable pride, Walter Jones acknowledges his membership in two of the more prominent groups:

I belonged to the Masons and the Elks. That's what I belong to now. They been around here since the world been around.

Indeed, the many organizations that existed on Vinegar Hill generated a great deal of community pride. And then there were those occasions when historical figures graced the Hill neighborhood. Inge recounts how

Distinguished black leaders always stopped here in the '80s and the first of the 1900s—Dr. R. R. Moton, who succeeded Mr. Booker T. Washington at Tuskegee Institute, a lot of the instructors at Hampton. They would be house guests of my mother and father. I was a little boy, but I remember Booker Washington came here. He and my father were acquaintances from Hampton.

I remember my father told a little anecdote. The barbershop—Pollard's—Booker went down there to get a shave. My father had an idle moment, and he went down there to see who was shaving that day, and told him, said, "You know who you're shaving?" Told him he was shaving Booker Washington. And he kinda laughed, and jumped, and was so shocked at who he was, my father had to say, "Hey, watch man you don't cut the man's throat!" They all used straight razors then, you know.

Laura Franklin also remembers being told of Washington's visit:

There used to be, right next to Mr. Inge's store, a barbershop run by a colored man, Mr. Wash Pollard. And he had a helper in there named Mr. Clarence Cary. And I can remember that.

And my uncle said he was up there one day getting his hair cut, and a man came in and said, "Mr. Inge?" They spoke to him and say—Well, my Uncle Nat say he knew him. So, Mr. Inge say, "Well, Booker T., how are ya?" And say, the barbershop man, he began to shake. And Tom Inge wrote up about his father, and he said that Booker T. Washington spent a night or two. They said he did. And Uncle Nat saw him. 'Cause my uncle went to Hampton.

Thomas Inge further reflects on the times during which his father owned Inge's Grocery:

In 1891, on the first day of July, Main Street—West Main—up there in the dock where my store is now, where my store was, was a moat road—no pavement—and in the early days, four-horse teams got stuck, and they had to bring two more horses from the livery stable to pull them out of the mud, right in front of his store. That's how long he had been there. All that time. And myself, I have seen oxen-drawn carts go by my store—my father's store rather—during my boyhood days.

George Ferguson gives additional description of those early years near the turn of the twentieth century.

The livery stable was the place where they kept horses, and you'd rent your horse and buggy. And you used to rent a stall and stored your horse there. It's been 59 or 60 years ago.

The railroad station has always been there since I can remember. At that time, C & O tracks were on the side they are now, and the Southern tracks were on the side that they are. And the trains from the West coming in on the C & O would stop up there and load and unload, and then they would go to the downtown station and stop and unload and load. Same with the trains going west.

I had an uncle who was a Pullman porter. And when he was coming from the West, I would go up there and meet him. And then I'd ride on the train down to the lower station and then walk home. At that time, you had what you call draymen or transfer men. They would meet all the trains and pick up all the luggage and distribute it where it had to go. That was in horse-and-wagon days.

Lionel Key elaborates on how transportation developed from horse-drawn vehicles to electrically powered streetcars.

Back in before the turn of the century, we had cars on Main Street, horse-drawn cars on Main Street. They, I believe, started at the old C & O depot at the end of East Main Street, came up Main Street to about Ninth Street, and went out Ninth Street on out what was called the Dummy Line, and on into Frye Springs.

They were later replaced with electric streetcars. I don't know what year they came into existence, but in my recollection, I've seen reports that were somewhere before 1900, probably '97, '98. They operated along Main Street—the C & O depot on up Main Street into Jefferson Park Avenue. They wired off. One branch went to Frye Springs. Another went to the university, up Rugby Road, up to the C & O railroad tracks. At the end of the tracks on Rugby Road they had a turntable, and when the car got to the end of the line, then the motorman would get out, push, turn the car around on the turntable. You'd have to get out, push it. The car would turn around on the turntable.

They traveled on the high part of Rugby Road, off of the paved part along where the sidewalk is on Rugby between Main Street and the bridge. That tie right there is where the cars operated in those days. But they were on Main Street next to the university wall, in that area coming down the street, until they came out onto the 14th Street bridge.

They were approximately in the Seventh Street area, around down into town, with meeting points at several locations—one at Jefferson Park and Main Street. The cars met there. Then, on the old Southern bridge was a meeting point. At Ridge and Main there was a meeting point down on what is now the mall, in front of the theater there. Used to be the Jefferson Theatre. There was also a meeting point between First and Second Street East. So, there were several places the cars would meet, one going one way and then the other.

One can sense in Key's recapitulation a regret that the socioeconomic progress of the black neighborhood did not keep pace with the city's industrial breakthroughs.

What indeed should have been done about Vinegar Hill with its historical vestiges that included living standards ranging from virtual shacks to well-constructed stately buildings? The city opted for total clearance. But Key suggests that selective renovation might have been a better approach.

I never did think that it was that bad. Of course, I know a lot of the houses were deteriorated in the area that's off of Main Street. And some of the houses on Main Street were not in the best repair. But there were some fairly good, what I considered good, buildings along Main Street that could have been brought up to certainly safe standards, if they were unsafe, without having to tear them down. There were other places back on Commerce and Williams Street, with some work could have been in good shape.

There were two churches torn down, one on Commerce Street and one on Fourth Street, that were removed in the redevelopment area. One on Fourth Street moved out on Preston Avenue not too far from Rugby Road. The other one, I'm not sure whether it continued to operate or not. But I think we could have rehabilitated a whole lot, without as much money. We certainly wouldn't have had as much vacant land.

In mentioning "vacant land," Key refers to the seven acres of the Hill that remained no more than a grassy slope, 20 years after the initial clearance had occurred. The fact that those acres were left empty so long has prompted some people to conclude that the city, in implementing urban renewal, was concerned about only one thing, removing blacks from the area. This is what Sadie Mason, a former teacher at Jefferson School, believes:

Residential area of Vinegar Hill in the early 1960s before renewal. (Some houses in standard condition are shown.) (Courtesy of the Charlottesville Department of Community Development).

We had no choice. We didn't have any choice at all. If they had improved the homes, we would've stayed there. If the homes had been improved, we would've stayed there, because we were close to where I worked—the Jefferson School. We didn't own any property there. We were renting. We had to go. No compensation whatsoever. I feel they should have done something. You just don't uproot people like that. Even when you're renting, you don't do things like that. I worked at Jefferson School, and Jefferson School was right down the hill. That's where I was educated, so that speaks for itself. It was not convenient at all. A whole complete new world. My husband had to go out and find some place for us to go.

In her interview, Mason pointed out that tenants were given one year to find new lodging. However, she would have stayed on Vinegar Hill if such had been an option.

In accordance with the governmental prerogative of eminent domain, renters were not compensated for the inconvenience of moving. Property owners were compensated, but even among them, Sherman White recalls that

The general attitude was one of reluctance, especially people who owned their property. They were very reluctant. Of course, the city came in with eminent domain and took the property. People who put their life savings in a home and then are suddenly faced with having to leave that home are only going to get back a pittance, you know, in terms of what they sunk into it, to relocate. Trying to replace their home with a similar home out in the community was a real strain. Just think of it. These people had already paid for one home. Now here they are in their 50s, 60s, and 70s, and you ask them to pay for another one. You know, it really was a hardship.

This large section of Vinegar Hill had been left vacant as late as the early 1980s.

Raymond Bell remembers tenants who enjoyed where they lived on the Hill and were deeply saddened when they were forced to move.

The black families that had to move out of the Vinegar Hill section, most of them— I would say 95 or 98 percent of them—did not want to move because they liked where they lived. They had roots there. They had—Half their families had been born in that area. These were families that had been there for two or three generations, kids that we grew up with. And they were just removed. And those people, many who had no means to buy a home, had to go to Hardy Drive, to the projects. Some of the old people that lived in that area. There was a lady I remember who moved over to Hardy Drive, and all she talked about was not having a place to plant little flowers or plant little gardens. She couldn't do that in the projects. So, it had its toll from an economic point of view, and it also had its toll—man's inhumanity to man, when you think of what it did in terms of uprooting families.

Laura Franklin explains the circumstances of her two elderly aunts, one of whom died as a result of having to move.

When my aunt—that was when they were condemning that area and going to move it down. Well, my aunt didn't want to move, and she would rather die than to move, and she did. The Lord took her. But she was 82.

Franklin continues:

Federal courthouse under construction in the early 1980s.

But my other aunt, she didn't die, but she worried all the time. She was over here. She always wanted to walk around there and see it. It was terrible that she had to move.

Some of the people that lived from Main Street all the way down to the bank, that was a whole area of houses. They didn't want to move. But when they laid prices, they got lost because they thought that they should've been paid more money. And most of those people are up in the projects now, because they built that place and moved them up there. And my aunt could have gone over there, but she didn't want to go over there.

It is debatable whether homeowners on the Hill were adequately compensated for their loss of property. Franklin, for example, gives the following details of an encounter at city hall:

This lady was down there at city hall that day when I was down there. And she said she fixed up her home right much and she hated to move. And she didn't think she really got her worth out of it.

Edward Jackson, a grandson of Nannie Cox Jackson, agrees that the amount of compensation was inadequate.

They took about 20 pieces of property from us in the area. And, of course, inflation was not like it is now. But I still think it was very, very low prices.

One of Nannie Cox Jackson's granddaughters, Teresa Price, offers further insight with regard to the compensation issue.

I don't think anybody feels that they are fairly compensated for loss of property, because they feel that that real estate will give them a good return on their investment. My family owned property on the main street of Vinegar Hill and in the residential section of Vinegar Hill, which was Third Street, that was Third Street and Commerce Street. The real estate value on our houses was not very much. And so, they were compensated— During eminent domain, they compensate people in terms of the value of the real estate in city hall. And when you get that compensation, we don't get enough to reinvest it in what you would call a better kind of real estate. So, they didn't feel like they were ever adequately compensated. My family owned the property where city hall is and I don't remember whether or not at that point that they felt that was an adequate price in terms of what you get for real estate now. But as to whether or not they complained a great deal, as you look back on them now, I would say that they were extremely agreeable, because they seemed to feel that whatever the city wanted to do was for progress and they must cooperate. They just went along with the plan. They didn't complain.

The Reverend Hall, who would become a member of the city council in the 1980s long after the decision in favor or urban renewal had been made, reveals the circumstances of a member of his congregation and notes the distrust with which most blacks viewed Charlottesville city administrators.

Sister Lucy Wiggins, she had a lovely home. When she died, she died here about four years ago, she was still paying a mortgage on the house that she built in another section. So, people like that got some money but not enough to get the type of house that they would have wanted. A lot of these people bought their homes when they were much younger. A lot of them in their 60s and 70s, so they're trapped. Instead of building back on Vinegar Hill, as it was told to them, they went over and built over on Hardy Drive, put up so many units over there, and bade the people in and said, "Now you can go into these houses and you can rent according to your income." And a lot of the people fell for that and now they're locked in. It's certainly affected the people's attitudes toward anything that the city will try to do. Each meeting we get into about some plans what we're going to do, they say, "Uh-uh, it's gonna be just like Vinegar Hill. You took our houses from us, especially the older people, and we ended up over in the projects." And that's where some of them are and some of them will die. That's what they do.

Interestingly enough though, Edward Jackson's brother, William, believes that the move to public housing was beneficial to those who had formerly been renting on the Hill.

I don't think you could have expected the people that owned that property there, with the rent they were getting from that property, to have been able to improve it to a place where they could have really gotten much better rent than they got. So, in point

Teresa Price and William Jackson (Courtesy of the Charlottesville Department of Community Development).

of living arrangements, I think it was an improvement. People got more modern housing with running water inside and that sort of thing.

And indeed there is evidence that at least some of the homeowners on the Hill were satisfied with the move. Says Ferguson,

Some of those people who had homes went into debt to get a new home. But all of them that I know have very nice new homes, very nice homes.

Thomas Johnson declares,

I was talking to a lady who had lived next door to us. And she couldn't wait to get out of that area. She was just anxious when the city came through saying, "We're going to tear down all these houses, and you're going to have to move." She bought a beautiful home too. It's just as you go around the curve up here.

A major issue still remains, however, concerning whether it would have been feasible to renovate some of the houses. The Reverend Benjamin Bunn is ambivalent.

I think the decision to revitalize it was good. I am not qualified to decide categorically whether it should have been a total demolition as it was, or whether there should have been some selected reconstruction.

Gene Arrington, the housing director, insists that no urban renewal program has succeeded when it comprised partial clearance and partial rehabilitation.

Robert Weaver, the nation's first black secretary of housing and urban development, elaborates on the complications:

> Rehabilitation in the gray areas will continue to present problems and its progress will be difficult.... Rehabilitation will be complicated by the hesitancy of local renewal officials to undertake it and the tendency of the Federal Housing Administration to resist new principles of underwriting. The hesitancy of the local officials will reflect two principal situations: The opposition to redirecting a program and the greater effort required to carry out rehabilitation as contrasted to clearance.... My experience suggests that if rehabilitation is approached as a practical rather than an ideological issue, results can be obtained. But the case-by-case approach is time-consuming and frequently frustrating.[13]

Evidently, federal policy makes it simpler to get funding in cases where total clearance is the goal. A house-by-house approach would have been extremely difficult, but perhaps most effective in terms of helping citizens who were in danger of losing the most. Then again, the issue might not so much have been one involving too much time and frustration if what the city was really concerned about was just how to get control of the Vinegar Hill area regardless of the fact that some of the structures conformed to the standard housing codes.

One understands therefore how some of the blacks might have difficulty assessing the overall Vinegar Hill project. Thomas Johnson, who at one time said homeowners got an advantage, is now not exactly sure.

I would say it was effective to the good of some people, the conditions that some of the people were living in. And others, particularly the older people, I feel that they had worked hard all their lives and built their home. And I feel that they were just told, "Okay, you got to move. That's it! No questions asked. We gonna pay you for your house. Whatever we can give you for it, you got to take it."

I think that was wrong. Because like I said, working hard all your life to buy a home, get it paid for, and then somebody come along and say, "I'm sorry, but you got to move." I mean in some ways it was good for some people, and for others, it just wasn't.

Raymond Bell conveys an even deeper skepticism.

They tell you, "We're trying to renovate." It came along with urban redevelopment. And, of course, we refer to it as urban removal of black people. And I may be paranoid about the subject, but I've always thought that that Vinegar Hill thing was by design to get rid of black businesses along that street, along Main Street. I still believe that this was a way the city and the state and people could get together and just get all the niggers away from that section.

Sadie Mason echoes that sentiment.

The homes were bad everywhere, all over town. You can walk around Charlottesville, and the homes are bad everywhere. But if they could have brought those people back, a lot of those people would be living today. Because that was home to them. And I'm for the aged people. And that was home to them.

You understand what I'm trying to get to you? Okay. If they could put homes there, all that empty space there—Plus, they were going to put up buildings. I think it was a political and a money thing for the white man. And I'm going to speak and tell you like it is because they wanted to get blacks from down there.

So, they put them in—But if they'd just put homes down there at the end, after they'd cleaned up all that down there, so we could've gone back. And I would've gladly gone back and paid the rent. I don't care who's listening to it, but I'm going to tell it like it is.

The fact remains that during the late 1950s and the early 1960s, whites controlled city government and owned most of the lucrative businesses. Indeed there was little that blacks could do to influence public policies even if the policies impacted primarily upon them. Urbanologist Jeanne Lowe comments on the prospect of hidden agendas:

> Some communities seemed to regard redevelopment as a way of dispersing their city's mounting number of Negroes. By 1964, some 63 percent of the families relocated from Title I areas were non-white, so it is not surprising that slum clearance came to be labeled "Negro clearance," and urban renewal as "Negro removal...." The fact that residents were often the last to be brought into project plans, and only to be told they would have to move soon, fostered the bitterness with which many people came to regard urban redevelopment. The result of such relocation practices was often to spread slum conditions.[14]

Lionel Key believes that many properties on the Hill only needed renovation. Still, he gives the city the benefit of the doubt as far as what might have been the motive for total clearance.

I thought a lot of the places could have been rehabilitated, at a lot less cost.... They wanted to improve the life of the people living in the area. They thought that by tearing down so-called slums, put them in better living conditions, it would improve their living conditions.

And so, the debate continues concerning whether or not the move to Westhaven was conducted with the best interests of the black community in mind. What we do know, however, is that ghetto conditions have developed in the housing project. Lowe points out that some people "blamed urban renewal itself for causing and not curing these social problems, and even called for a halt to the program."[15] When one considers the prospect that renewal might actually cause circumstances for many to get worse and not better, it is indeed good to rethink the methodology of such programs and learn from previous errors.

A change in governmental perspective was certainly evident in Charlottesville when another substantially black neighborhood, Starr Hill, became targeted in the late 1970s for urban renewal. The objective of that project was rehabilitation of the already existing structures instead of total demolition. Bell explains how that particular project was different:

It was a grant for the renovation of dilapidated housing, to do some things cosmetically in terms of painting houses. They gave free paint to businesses and residential homeowners, to paint. They put sidewalks down, lighting, planted trees on West Main Street. Along the West Main Street corridor, right above the Vinegar Hill section, you had old stores closing down. So, the city made a proposal for the grant, and they got something like, I think, two million dollars.

This time there would be no confiscation of private property, no governmental reliance on eminent domain. Sadie Mason wishes that such a plan had been implemented for Vinegar Hill and that if houses had to be destroyed, they could have been replaced right there in the same location.

If they had put homes down there, instead of what they did, if they had put homes down there, I'd be living down there today. I think it was awful. I'm speaking for me, okay. I don't know about the others. I'm speaking for myself.

A question remains, however, concerning whether the strategies that were employed on Starr Hill in the 1970s would have been effective on Vinegar Hill in the 1950s and 1960s. In *The Rough Road to Renaissance*, Jon Teaford assesses the implementation of urban renewal in four major cities — Baltimore, Detroit, Philadelphia, and St. Louis. In particular, Teaford stresses that at a certain point, city administrators concluded that selective rehabilitation would be a more effective strategy than wholesale clearance. It had been concluded that the circumstances of society's dispossessed had not been significantly improved through previous clearance plans in spite of the millions of dollars that had been funneled into those operations.

Committed to a new direction, Philadelphia launched a "leadership program" in 1954 that aimed to encourage grassroots leaders to organize residents of the renewal areas for greater involvement of those who would be most affected by whatever plan was finally chosen. One might suppose that such a strategy would have been useful during the era of urban renewal on Vinegar Hill. Whites controlled the city council, whites controlled the Charlottesville Redevelopment and Housing Authority, and prominent white businessmen had a significant voice in determining what would become of the Vinegar Hill black community. The probability is great that if blacks had had anything close to substantial control over the situation, selective rehabilitation as opposed to total clearance would have been the ultimate consensus.

Yet administrators in those other cities learned that "the positive consequences of rehabilitation proved fleeting, for despite a new coat of paint and mended window screens, the deterioration of aging structures continued."[16] Of course, the rehabilitation efforts in those cities involved much more than just applying a fresh coat of paint and mending window screens. Often entire windows were replaced, as well as doors. Roofs and porches were repaired, trash was removed, and attempts were made to slow down in general the problematic property deterioration that existed in the urban renewal locations. But those efforts served only a cosmetic purpose, and city officials ultimately assessed rehabilitation as having been unsuccessful.

Much of the difficulty with rehabilitation in those other instances centered around whether residents could afford to maintain their premises after government assistance programs had ended. And certainly, neither local nor federal government agencies were willing to commit themselves indefinitely to rehabilitation funding. So poverty became the key issue. The Starr Hill project involved only a few blocks of Charlottesville where most of the residents and proprietors were financially secure enough to benefit from the government boost and then perpetuate the rehabilitation advantages. But such was not the situation with the aforementioned renewal projects in Baltimore, Detroit, Philadelphia, and St. Louis. In those cities the areas that were in need of rehabilitation were much more extensive, and the residents in general were living in dire straits.

So, even as Ray Bell, Sadie Mason, and others express regret that rehabilitation was not implemented on Vinegar Hill along the lines of what later occurred on Starr Hill, one cannot be certain that rehabilitation would have been the answer either. At times it seems as if a curse has been put on the overwhelming majority of the black race. Making our way off the plantations after slavery, we ventured into nearby southern towns, forced to accept whatever housing was available in the limited locations that were designated for us. Except for a few, we mostly continued our menial labor, eking out a living that was better than slavery, hopefully at least in the psychological sense. Financially though, we remained at the lowest rungs, our destinies tied as much to that as to any other sociological factor.

CHAPTER FIVE

THE IMPACTS OF URBAN RENEWAL

Employment and Black Businesses

Vinegar Hill was once a monument to the persistence of a people who were forced to endure the pain of being discriminated against on a regular basis. Although different economic classes existed there, most people were engaged in domestic labor and other low-paying jobs. Walter Jones compares the employment limitations that existed then to the increased opportunities of more contemporary times.

It's hard to get somebody to do a lot of domestic work now. But all down through the years, that's all that they could do before all these jobs opened up to these. And then, I tell you the reason for that too. The generation has changed, and people are preparing themselves more for the better jobs. They are more qualified to hold different jobs. More people are doing that. Because at first they didn't have a chance. If they had prepared themselves for these particular jobs, they wouldn't have been able to get them anyway.

Lionel Key tells how some blacks worked for the railroad companies whereas others owned barbershops or worked, as Jones pointed out, in the lower echelons.

The C & O. There were some with the Southern. They were scattered through the city government. City Public Works Department had a number of them. The Gas Department had many, and some other jobs. I don't believe there were any department heads at that time that were black, in the city. But there were many of them employed by the city and many by the university, as they are now. There were a lot of black people employed at the hospital and other jobs around the university. Some of them were employed by the fraternities at the university, and there was a black barbershop for whites at the university. A couple of Browns, the Brown brothers operated that barbershop those years back.

Thomas Inge, whose father went to school with Booker T. Washington, praises that college president's philosophy in light of what the employment opportunities were for those who lived on the Hill.

Booker T. Washington helped us out a lot, although the black people don't give him credit. You, everybody can't be a professor, a professional man, a doctor, or a lawyer, or a degreed man. Somebody's got to lay the brick, and somebody's got to mix the mortar, and somebody's got to pour the cement and do cement work. And Booker Washington believed in having men trained to do that. Somebody had to do the farming. He didn't believe in having every man go and try to farm. He believed in training man to farm, make it sound technically, and then go out and farm. And a lot of people don't understand that about him. They just say he didn't want Negroes to do nothing but farm, use their hands. But he wanted them trained to do it, and that's where the difference is.

W. E. B. Du Bois, of course, disagreed with the notion that that was the best direction for blacks to take in pursuit of social progress. He believed that the Tuskegee president was trying to hold the black race back: "Mr. Washington represents in Negro thought the old attitude of adjustment and submission; but adjustment at such a peculiar time as to make his programme unique. This is an age of unusual economic development, and Mr. Washington's programme naturally takes an economic cast, becoming a gospel of Work and Money to such an extent as apparently almost completely to overshadow the higher aims of life."[1] In explaining the nature of the employment diversity that existed on Vinegar Hill, George Ferguson in some sense reconciles Washington's and Du Bois's philosophies.

There were a lot of people that did domestic work, a lot of people that did—that worked at the university—custodial work, and people who worked in dining rooms, hotels. And there were people who, as I said, were draymen, people who hauled things, you know, had the horse and wagons and would haul things. And people did custodial work, those types of jobs.

We've never had a large professional group here in Charlottesville. We had another black physician that came here in 1913. As I understand it, there was one—before he came here—who left. We had a black dentist that came here in 1913. Then we had another black dentist that came here in 1923. Charlottesville, up until recently, has always supported two or three black physicians, and it supported two black dentists.

Organizations such as the National Negro Business League, which Washington organized in 1900, were instrumental in getting new businesses started, but one wonders whether such organizations were actually able to overcome what historian Jay Mandle has called the lingering "plantation structure":

> Self-help and the creation of a class of black businessmen represent at least
> a potential means for some blacks to overcome plantation-induced poverty.

Even aside from the limited numbers who could benefit, however, there was a major weakness in this approach. The success of self-help ultimately depended not only on the blacks successfully endowing themselves with skills, but also on the creation of opportunities for the skills to be put to profitable use. But there was nothing in the strategy that spoke to this problem, for ultimately the limited opportunities available to blacks in the South were a function of the plantation structure.[2]

It was segregation in the first place that actually facilitated the dependence of blacks upon each other for the exchange of goods and services. But in analyzing Mandle's intriguing perspective, one is forced to contemplate exactly where prior self-help methods, caused by that segregation, have led blacks in more modern times. Raymond Bell, for one, believes that the general economic plight of blacks in Charlottesville has actually gotten worse.

You had more, even more in terms of economic development, in those days than you have today. We're losing that economic development that we used to have.

We've got to get back into it because when I was coming along, my father, as I mentioned, was the first black to own a funeral home. Dr. Jackson was the first black to have a dentist's office here. When he died, two of his sons got in it. He had a stroke. He was practicing, but his father started that business.

We are second-generation businessmen. You see, so you had that, and you had black physicians—Dr. Johnson who lived next to Dr. Jackson. We had, at that time, two black physicians. There was a Dr. Ferguson, the father of George Ferguson who has a funeral home here now. Dr. Ferguson was the first black physician. But today, you don't have a black physician in town as far as practicing. We don't have but one black dentist in town.

In those days when Vinegar Hill had good income for shopowners, you didn't have those large supermarkets like you have today, like Safeway. So, Mr. Inge's grocery store, that's when I was a child, that's where my father did all of his grocery shopping. We would go there on Saturday night, and he might spend $15 and he'd have two wagons full of food for $15. Mr. Inge sold chickens and anything you'd need. He had live chickens, live turkeys, live ducks. And we would go over there to do all of our shopping. And many black families would. He sold fish. It was the only fish market in town. And those businesses were very viable businesses.

And much to the director of housing's chagrin, there were families not in the grocery business who were intent nonetheless on being self-sustaining to the point that they raised their own livestock. Laura Franklin states that

When I was a little girl, down there with my people, we had pigs in the backyard, in the garden, in the pigpen. And they had to feed chickens. And we had one chicken we called "Dickey B." He didn't have many feathers on him. We had cows, chickens, and everything in the yard, extending from the Main Street all the way down. So, we had something like a farm. But it was small, not like a huge farm.

Drusilla Hutchinson tells how her family provided stock for Inge's Grocery.

Mr. Inge, his father opened that place. And I used to go there when I was just a girl with my father. His father used to buy live chickens, and he used to buy rabbits from us. And daddy used to twist tobacco. We raised a little tobacco. He had a lot of old men that chewed tobacco, and they liked twisted tobacco. And we used to stop there, and I used to catch rabbits and trap them because he liked trapped rabbits. Well, when he died, his son took over.

George Ferguson remembers hunting season.

A lot of people, men went hunting. Didn't never hear too much of fishing because we weren't surrounded by any water. But they did quite a bit of hunting here, in the hunting season. At that time, buy rabbits from stores. You would come down the street, and they would have a string of rabbits hanging down. About this time of the year you'd buy rabbits, and you could buy fresh pork. People would slaughter the hogs, and the stores would buy. You know, you'd have that in the stores. They worked hard, and went to bed early and got up early.

Needless to say, those days were not destined to last forever. Former Secretary of Labor Ray Marshall, in studying the employment patterns of blacks in the South, came to the following conclusion:

> The traditional nonagricultural employment pattern for blacks in the South was to be restricted to menial or otherwise disagreeable jobs, except for some professional and skilled positions in black communities. There were few exceptions where blacks were able to penetrate better jobs (such as bricklaying in the construction industry) because they had learned these occupations as slaves, and techniques were sufficiently stable that whites could not freeze them out by monopolizing the latest technology.[3]

Marshall gave particular attention to the 1960s, the same period of time during which the Hill was undergoing renewal. Though blacks at that point may not have been completely "frozen out" of the construction industry, they were clearly the victims of an exclusionary ploy when it came to the barbering business. As George Ferguson explains:

There was only one barbershop that was run by a white man for whites. The rest of the barbershops, that were frequented by whites, were run for whites, but run by blacks. They had barbershops up the university, up on West Main Street, and downtown. They were trained to cut it, and they made, those men made a decent living, a good living, running those barbershops. But then the white man found out that there was a piece of living in operating a barbershop, and they started passing those laws. You see, before then, you could come and work for me, and I would teach you how to be a barber. You may not be able to read and write, but you could be a good barber. But then they passed laws where you had to take an examination, and the white barbers—These white shops started opening up.

The former NAACP president continues with his description of the process whereby many black barbers were systematically put out of business.

You could become a barber by serving your apprenticeship under another barber. And you would learn the trade that way. And then, of course, they started getting this licensing thing, and it made it more difficult. But those who were already in business were saved. But this was one way of getting them out. They had a number of shops, small shops around here, and they made a very good business, had a very good business. Most men at that time got a shave in the barbershop, so they really went to the barbershop nearly every day and so forth.

They had black barbershops too. This Pollard barbershop that I mentioned on Main Street was for blacks. There was a Mr. White's barbershop on Main Street that was for blacks.

They had a number of shops here. Had one up in the university, right up there, you know, when you go up the steps on the Charlottesville side. You go up Main Street, and then you go up steps to Anderson's Bookstore. It was a lucrative business, so much so that the state barbers association got together and passed laws that a person had to get a license and take a test to become a barber. And this began pushing the black businesses out.

By the 1960s black businesses also had to contend with the modernization of equipment, as well as the increased industrialization of business enterprises as a whole. Ruth Coles, for example, recalls what contributed to the decline of her father's barbering business:

Of course, when the electric razors and all those things came into being, men did not have to go to the barbershop every morning before they went to their businesses. Then, black barbershops, that type of barbershop sort of passed out.

And such increased industrialization can also be blamed in part for speeding up the demise of Inge's Grocery. Thomas Inge thinks that

The biggest thing that has hurt black businesses is the chain-store business, when the chain store began, so numerous now and so close together until they are cutting each other's throat now, and it's just no place. My father told me years ago, before he died, that in a few years, a small black business is going to be almost a thing of the past because they cannot meet the competition.

I did very well when I first took my father's store over. I was open at eight o'clock in the morning, or before eight, and stayed there until eleven o'clock at night. But now all of the chain stores are staying open until eleven, a lot of them all night long, and so they cut all of that out. And I never would accept Sunday hours. I never established Sunday hours, but the chain stores, they even stay open all day Sundays, some of them, and you can't beat that kind of competition to save your life. Towards the last, it got where I could go down to the chain store and buy certain commodities, to sell in my store, cheaper than I could buy them from the local wholesale dealer.

Down there at Hampton where my brother used to live, they had a black co-op, and in this black co-op, all the black people, who loved it, encouraged him to buy there. But I think that thing finally went out of business. They couldn't meet the change or competition any better than anyone else did. Can't nobody meet it.

**Thomas Inge (Courtesy of the Char-
lottesville Department of Community
Development).**

*Take the people like the A & P.
They own their own canneries. They
own their own bakeries. They buy a little of these other brands of stuff that
they have in there because some people
insist on having it. But the biggest
bundle in their business is they own the
factories and the industries that's putting
the cans out, and everything else. Ain't
no use in thinking you can beat that
kind of competition because you can't do
it. And you can luck up and get a location maybe somewhere where you do
well, but the average place, you just
cannot meet it.*

In spite of not being able to compete
effectively with the supermarket phenomenon, Inge continued operation
of the corner store that his father had
started in 1891. Located on the extreme
southwest edge of Vinegar Hill, it
barely escaped the urban renewal
demolition. During its peak years the store not only served the black community, but it had major contracts with the Clermont and Gleason Hotels, the
Dolly Madison Inn, the University of Virginia Hospital, and boarding houses
in the university area. When he closed his doors for the last time in 1979, the
building was designated an historic landmark, a fitting tribute to what had
been for so long a prominent feature of the city's landscape. Inge reminisces
about the crucial contemporary social changes and the circumstances that led
to his father's entrepreneurial venture in the first place.

*I just hung on there until after the supermarkets began to get closer and closer and com-
petition got keener and keener. But business turned out smaller and smaller. So, toward
the last, I wasn't making any money. But I was enjoying it, being there and meeting
the people and talking. Everybody knows who's in this town, the older people anyhow.
So, I enjoyed that, and I think my wife kind of enjoyed that too. She came there after
my mother died, and worked with me and father. And after my father died—before he
died, three or four years before he died—she and I took over the business, and we ran it
until we closed on the 31st of October in nineteen and seventy-nine....*

*At the time when my father, George P. Inge, came to Charlottesville, he taught
in the public schools, and he taught for several years. And he had a first grade, what
they call a first grade certificate. And his salary was the top salary at that time, which
was $28 a month. He saw no future in that, so he resigned from the school system,*

Inge's Grocery Store (Courtesy of the Charlottesville Department of Community Development).

sent in his resignation. And the superintendent begged him to teach one more year. They were building the old Jefferson School that has been torn down now, and the superintendent wanted him to at least teach that one more year. And he told him, "No, I finished. I made up my mind, and it's final." And he opened that business. And after that, he enjoyed a very successful business.

Ferguson gives more details of the changes brought on by industrialization.

The entrance of chain stores like Safeway and A & P. And this was when I was a child. Now, the Inge's store was one of the thriving stores in the community. They had delivery and everything. You had about three or four grocery stores that were owned and operated by blacks, but with the Depression and the opening up of the chain store—And you had several white stores that were owned by individuals. But with the opening up of chain stores, that type of thing phases out.

And we had some beauticians and seamstresses. We had some launderers, but see, all of that type of thing is gone with the new inventions. Now, I can't find anybody that irons my shirts like I want them. All of that is gone with the new inventions.

Was it really urban renewal that spelled the end for so many black businesses in Charlottesville? Or was the small business owner, of the sort that once existed on Vinegar Hill, destined for extinction long before even a single building had been torn down?

The Black Family and Social Organizations

Ruth Coles, a retired schoolteacher, notes that the church played a significant role, sponsoring events at which Vinegar Hill residents could spend their leisure time.

We had a lot of activities in our churches. We went in for plays and things of that sort.

Coles then adds this qualification:

We had a great family life, so no one was looking for any leisure.

Family stability existed in great measure for those who lived on the Hill. That was to be expected from middle-class families such as the one into which Coles was born. But even poor families possessed values that many people today would envy.

And then there is Alies Jones who had spoken earlier about borrowing wood or coal or coffee, of people waking up in the morning and, right off the bat, going over to check and make sure that a neighbor was doing okay. Jones tells of the time when she was bedridden with a prolonged illness.

I was sick. I was sick a long time. It was just like one big family. Everybody down there was one big family.

On Vinegar Hill the concept of "family" extended beyond family members. The feeling was much more expansive and especially included giving help to a neighbor in need.

Fraternal organizations and federated women's clubs, such as those mentioned in chapter four, also embodied the "family" spirit. These organizations provided services that otherwise might not have been available to the black community. Crisis intervention, academic scholarships, and theatrical productions are but a few of the services that such organizations contributed to the Hill's enhancement. But as Edward Jackson reminds us, it was during urban renewal that

They displaced the Masons. And they were on Vinegar Hill.

Even Thomas Inge, who never bothered to join such organizations, nonetheless acknowledges their importance to the residents of Vinegar Hill.

They had a lot of literary clubs, social and literary clubs. But they were women's clubs, now what they call the federated clubs. They had a lot of those there. My father was quite a staunch Mason, but I never joined any secret organization to this day because I just wasn't inclined to be interested in fraternal organizations. They had their place in the community, and they developed a lot of talent in the community. And a lot of men developed through those organizations.

That those groups could be so successful has to do, in part, with how the general society had shunted blacks off into isolated settings with comparatively limited resources. Individuals coming together to pool their various skills and ideas was one way that the limitations were sometimes overcome.

Crime

Serious crime rarely ever occurred on the Hill. Drusilla Hutchinson lived on West Main Street for a decade:

I could walk up and down the street. I never had any trouble. Lunchrooms and stores and colored people all there, and I never had none. I used to walk up and down there, and I had to come home at night. I used to have to come up there eight, sometimes nine o'clock, and I never did have any trouble with anybody. No, we didn't have any trouble whatsoever when I lived up on Vinegar Hill. I used to could take my children out walking and everything. I never had anybody to say anything to me, and I always treated everybody nice, and everybody always treated me nice.

Connie Brooks agrees:

We used to leave our doors open, our windows open. Nobody never bothered us. We wouldn't think of anything happening. Breaking in your house? It never happened.

I used to come from New York when I was in my teens, and I'd walk, you know, where the train station is. I'd walk all the way up in this area. Nobody ever tried to rob me. Never. They were poor, but they never thought of it. You could walk any time of night. Nobody would bother you.

Cora Anderson, who did missionary work and sold insurance on the Hill, also remembers that it was safe enough for women to walk there at night.

You could walk anywhere, because when I was carrying insurance I could be up at night collecting insurance and nobody would ever bother me. But you couldn't do that now…. Any night you wanted to go to missionary and you wanted to walk over town and walk back, women alone, it didn't make any difference because wasn't nobody going to bother you, you see. But you see how things have changed.

Commora Snowden concurs:

I can't think of any problem with walking the streets at night, because in those days there was nothing you had to worry about…. We weren't worried about somebody breaking in the house. The people that I knew didn't lock their doors.

This is not to say that the peace was always kept. Bell, for example, admits that on certain occasions there was a degree of rowdiness.

Now in some areas of Vinegar Hill, there was a place that you had quite a bit of Saturday night ruckus going on and people drinking, you know, too many beers and having fights and some shootings. That happened in Tonsler's poolroom, because you had young guys who'd work all week, and they wanted to, you know, "get down" on Saturday night. And they would get down on Vinegar Hill. So, it got a reputation of being kind of a bad place.

It wasn't all that bad, because I used to go over there to get my hair cut there. My father, when I was a young kid, would drop me off at a barbershop, and he'd leave me there. So, I wasn't afraid, but the whites were afraid. Well, in walking down the street, they would cross over to the south side of Vinegar Hill so that they wouldn't, the white women wouldn't be whistled at or talked at or something, you see.

They saw it as an opportunity to say this is urban, ha-ha, renewal and housing redevelopment. So, they just picked that section. And they did it not only in Charlottesville, they did it all over.

The crime in Vinegar Hill—if you want to call it crime—was no more than raising hell on Saturday nights. And there were occasionally guys in the poolroom that would have too much to drink. And there were some shootings there and some cutting. But as far as stealing—going into a merchant's store and stealing things— you didn't have that in those days. I don't know why that is, but you just didn't have a big problem. You didn't have any break-ins the way you have today.

There used to be one guy that was a patrolman, a police named Dudley. And Dudley would walk, he had the Vinegar Hill beat, and he would walk from Tenth Street up here on, northwest down to the end of Vinegar Hill, Preston Avenue, one man. He was white. There were no black policemen in those days. Now, on Saturday nights, they wouldn't let Mr. Dudley walk that beat because he was too nice a police officer. They'd put a couple of tough guys in for him, couple of rednecks. And they would do that beat, and they would agitate, sometimes, the people who were out on the sidewalk—"Boy, move back," that kind of thing. And there were some "brothers" and "sisters" that would say, "I'm gonna do my thing on your policeman's head." And they would fight the policeman if they thought they were being harassed.

Edward Jackson's perspective is similar.

With the loitering crowd hanging out, the police were always out there. And there were people going downtown that would say they couldn't get on that side of the street....

They had a good time down there. That was the only place they had to go. It wasn't that bad, because I been out there, hanging around with them as a youngster. We didn't realize we were being that bad, but you have to have some outlet for people, and that was the only outlet they had in Charlottesville for a number of years, you know. And they had a lot of fun up there. I can tell you that.

Teresa Price, on the other hand, says that

It was kind of rough, I tell you. I used to walk on the other side of the street. My father owned the building, but we were not permitted to go in there because it was not considered a desirable place. I mean, not that we were being anything other than what we are. But, you know, it attracted certain people there that we were not expected to pattern ourselves after.

And Laura Franklin notes,

Yeah, my aunt always said this sure is a quiet street, because Fourth Street was a loud street. But people would run off of Vinegar Hill and be fighting and drunk and run right down to Fourth Street. People couldn't rest. Aunt Laura said she couldn't sleep.

According to Franklin, her aunt liked the place where she moved much more than her place on the Hill.

For others, there remain an ambivalence and a need to temper any criticism with the positive features of life in the neighborhood. Sherman White gives this account:

I think that everybody knew everybody. They had the kind of camaraderie where if one person's child got out of line, that neighbor had the right to correct him. I think that part of it was good.

Again too, it attracted a lot of undesirables as well. I think some people were glad to see it moved because it hopefully would remove an undesirable element. And other people were sorry to see it removed because it represented black history, black ownership. It represented some symbolic things to the black community.

Though she analyzes both sides of the situation, Rebecca McGinness is mainly defensive to the point of accusing the outside intervention.

There were rowdy spots and some good spots. They had businesses in there. Most of the black business was on the Hill—barbershops, restaurants, grocery stores, tailor shops, the pool hall. That's where most of the rowdiness was, in front of the pool hall.... But it was a neighborhood. People were good. I can see it through my eyes better than the white man can because I lived down there. The worst of it, as I can remember, was some portions of Third Street and some portions of Commerce, and the lower end of Fourth Street, northwest. But there wasn't anything but ordinary living. It wasn't a separate community like Westhaven is now.

I've lived in Charlottesville all my life. I'm right here to witness a whole lot of things. People were good. Parents had more control over their children then. Children didn't hang out around the poolrooms. Children weren't allowed on the Hill. Children played in the street or in the yard. See, some of the things you're hearing of those spots is through the eyes of whites. It wasn't as bad as it has been purported to be. Just plain God-fearing people. Everybody knew everybody else. Everybody knew everybody's children. If a child was rude, you went to the parents. People were good....

I don't think they were any dirtier than any other places we got up here. You could come through Main Street. I mean, I know what I'm talking about. The people had their restaurants down there. I didn't see a whole lot of trash like I see in a lot of these places right today. I didn't. I didn't see any trash. But regardless of all, I'm going to tell it like it is. A white man got tired of seeing all these people up on the street. I mean they weren't too violent. Wasn't nothing violent about it till some of them get too much in them, you know. Just like anything else. But Main Street wasn't all that dirty. Just the idea. So, you take it from there. The idea. Main Street wasn't all that dirty. Main Street wasn't as dirty as a whole lot of these places they got around here right now.

Rebecca McGinness (Courtesy of the Charlottesville Department of Community Development).

    Some people have given it a bad name and all. But a large number of the people down there owned their own homes. Some of the best colored people in town, families who were raised there. Good, beautiful homes. That has been the pattern of the average black person as far back as I can remember.

    There were some of them like that, rowdy and all. But, by and large, they were

Top: 1920 photograph of Jefferson School teachers (Front row: Maggie Terry, Maude Gamble, and Cora Duke. Second row: Ella Baylor, Rebecca McGinness, Peachie Jackson, Kathleen Chisholm, Carrie Michie, and Gertrude Inge. Third row: Nannie Cox Jackson, Marian Wyatt, Jane C. Johnson, and Helen Jackson) (Courtesy of the Jefferson School). *Bottom:* The new Jefferson School, now a day-care center for four-year-olds.

interspersed with a better class of black people who led respectable lives. I know. I taught those children. Schoolteachers visited the homes, and that had a big influence.

Some people worked in service for white people. A lot of them worked for the railroads. To a great extent, many of the women reared children. There were some schoolteachers lived there. Many of the women, although they stayed at home, they took in laundry and washed for the students at the university. The men worked laboring jobs.

It was a good relationship between people. Of course, there was segregation. You had to accept that as part of life.

McGinness portrays the Hill as a normal community, as normal in fact as any other black neighborhood might have been, functioning under similar circumstances. Yet if one is determined to uncover a major crime that occurred on the Hill, it perhaps would be best to consider the racism that was all too evident in Charlottesville. McGinness declares,

Black people were discriminated against. When the Jefferson Theatre was first built, black people had to buy their tickets around back. You had a special place where you could sit. In the gallery is where you sat. You couldn't sit on the first floor.... You couldn't go in any white restaurants. A man with a broom or a rolling pin would be in the door, telling you you couldn't come in because you were colored. And we couldn't go to the University of Virginia.

Hattie Bivens, who worked as a cook at Chris's Tavern on the Hill, describes the segregation at that establishment.

I worked at the tavern for 14 years, which was owned by a Greek but which I ran most of—a good part of it, which was divided into two sections, but not cut. You know, I mean you could walk from one section to the other with the white on one side and black on the other. And I ran the side for the black.

Walter Jones gives this account of another degrading situation:

At one time, they didn't allow blacks to play golf on the golf courses in this town. And I was the one that—in fact, it took me about two years—I started the fight with them, met with city council and all, in that golf. And I could only get it then for one day a week. We could go down to McIntire Park and play golf, on a same lane, one day a week. And they claimed that blacks weren't interested in golf. But I had been playing a long time, and going back and forth to Washington and playing at different places. And I felt like we shouldn't have done that. So, I started to fight with them. And I had one, a prosecuting attorney, tell me that he would turn the golf course into a cornfield before he let us play golf on it with them.

Even the most prominent blacks in America were subjected to this kind of treatment. No hotel would even admit the great black leader Booker T. Washington, who was compelled, when visiting Charlottesville, to join the Inges in living quarters above their grocery store. Thomas Inge conveys some of the sordid history.

My father, he went to Hampton. He and Booker T. Washington were there at the same time. They were friends, but not classmates. But he always kept in touch with Booker until he died. And Booker used to come to the store there when he was this way. In fact, he used to stop at this store there because blacks didn't have anywhere else to stop because, see, they couldn't get any accommodations at any hotels or motels or anything of that kind. He was always very highly respected, but he was black. And no blacks entered those hotels.

On another occasion, as Inge reports, a distinguished black musical quartet was forced to endure the segregation policy.

I have had experiences—me and my wife have been here—before these motels and hotels opened up. A quartet came and we took care of them. And the man who traveled with them, they went on these goodwill tours all through the North. He was white, and he stayed at the hotel. And he would come in here early in the morning and have breakfast with us and his quartet, and get on the road. But that quartet couldn't stay down there at that hotel.

Plessy v. Ferguson was the case that mandated separation of the races in public facilities. Citizens such as the Inges, through the use of their homes, were able to compensate for the regular inconvenience. But how does a society pay adequate compensation for a whole multitude of degrading experiences imposed on some of its members?

The Loss of Black Enterprise

In evaluating the overall impact of renewal on Vinegar Hill, it is necessary to consider several factors. Some residents lived in substandard housing. Others were indeed quite prosperous. What were the city's concerns? And now in retrospect, it is especially important to consider the long-term consequences of blacks having lost their entrepreneurial establishments. Charles Johnson, the undertaker who was unsuccessful in his bid to be a Democratic candidate in the 1960 city council election, asserts that

Numerically, we had more black businesses than we have now because at one time we had a drugstore, shoe repair shop, clothing store, barbershop, poolroom, restaurants. All of that, plus the Inge's Grocery Store which you notice is now closed. We had all of those black businesses in the Vinegar Hill area on Main Street. And with the urban renewal, all of them were put out of existence. We don't have any of those now.

Yes, the chain-store phenomenon was making inroads in Charlottesville at about the same time that renewal was taking place on the Hill. It surely would have driven some of the Hill entrepreneurs out of business. But all? White-owned businesses located on the Hill now seem to be doing quite well. And they certainly are not conglomerates. They have been able to prosper, to a large extent, because they are located right downtown.

In *The Impact of Urban Renewal on Small Business*, Brian Berry, Sandra Parsons, and Rutherford Platt raise the following issue:

> The crux of the matter is whether the liquidation rate among small business displacees is "excessive".... Losses are highest among food-related retail units, the smallest stores, stores whose owners entered business from the lowest socio-economic levels, and stores whose owners are closest to retirement. Yet these are the kinds of business declining most rapidly in the country at large. Does the high liquidation rate simply reflect national small business trends, perhaps with some hastening of the inevitable for a few, or is it greater among businesses dislocated by urban renewal than might reasonably have been expected if renewal had not taken place?...
>
> Small business is undergoing great changes because of increasing scale of retailing, increasing consumer mobility, and rising real incomes, all of which are contributing to the competitive success of large or more specialized retailing units and business centers, and the gradual elimination of those that are smaller and less viable.[4]

The point is thereby reiterated with regard to whether or not certain businesses would have "gone under" anyway even if renewal had never occurred. Those same authors, however, specify certain businesses as being in the most danger as a consequence of renewal projects:

1. Retail or service establishments dependent upon a particular neighborhood clientele dispersed as a result of urban renewal, especially in the case of neighborhoods with dominant ethnic or racial groups.
2. Marginal businesses which may or may not have been profitable.
3. Businesses whose owners retired, usually because of their age or lack of commercial enthusiasm.
4. Businesses for which no technical or specialized skills or knowledge were required.
5. Businesses with special licensing or franchise problems, such as liquor stores or automobile dealers.
6. Illegal businesses. No information is available about these, despite their significance during the pre-clearance stage and following the initial urban renewal announcements.[5]

Businesses that are illegal and unprofitable (and, to some extent, those businesses that are likely to end with their owner's retirement) are not the ones causing us to take issue with renewal as it occurred on Vinegar Hill. But what we wonder is whether tailors, barbers, insurance agents, and construction contractors, as they existed on the Hill, could have continued to prosper had it not been for the renewal process. Many of those businesses were not in any jeopardy at all.

Frank Henry, who started his barbershop on October 1, 1927, was opposed to renewal and now says this about the matter:

Frankly speaking, I didn't care much for it. I mean I don't care much for downtown now. You know, just personally speaking. Used to could see our people. See, now you—Of course, we were integrating and all of that....

There were electric cars at that time, and that was in '27. Streetcars were running all up and down the street. Right back of Mount Zion Church. It looked like they put the black people out of business, scattered them around. That's my personal opinion because it was more Negroes in business on Vinegar Hill than it is scattered through town.... You could meet people, that is, black people. We used to open up at nine o'clock in the morning on a Saturday and didn't leave until twelve or one o'clock at night.

Bell remembers that

There was a very fine unity and a very good feeling of comradeship and brotherhood in that area. If a black was having a problem, they'd help one another. Very good. And that type thing grew up over years. Actually you didn't have two blacks having the same type businesses in that area. So, they weren't competitors.

Actually, sometimes two or more black businesses were engaged in the same type of enterprise, as was the case with some of the barbershops and restaurants. But the nature of the competition (if it can even be called that) was nowhere near as cutthroat as it is today when businesses are located in the same neighborhood and are in pursuit of the same customers. On Vinegar Hill businesses that were engaged in similar enterprises helped each other succeed.

Edward Jackson, whose great uncle owned what was at one time the only outdoor sign company in America, offers additional insight as he raises the question considered earlier of whether or not at least some of the businesses could somehow have been preserved.

It has been a sort of sore spot with me, the taking of that property and the only black businesses that you really had, and not really going all out to help to at least establish or relocate one-for-one. In other words, if they took ten businesses, I think if they'd really been doing a good job, they would've made a great effort to help get ten more folks back in business.

Then another thing that has annoyed me is the fact that they never came back, to my knowledge, and offered any of that property back to blacks. When they were taking it, they said they would. When urban renewal was taking it, cleaning up, they said they would offer some of the property back to you, you know, if you wanted to open a business.

Sometimes you have to take a fellow by the hand and sort of lead him on, you know. I don't think any of that was done to show good intent. I worked very hard, trying to maybe get the McDonald's down there to be a black McDonald's. But the franchise was so high, it was almost impossible to raise the money to get it.

So, as I said, I hate to see the blacks put out of that property. And it looks like they're totally out of it now. And I don't feel that they paid fair prices for a lot of the property. Maybe some people got a fair price.

And then to let it sit there. And to show you that they didn't have a plan, and it's pretty close to true, that the thing that annoyed them, they didn't like Vinegar Hill sitting in the middle of the downtown business and University of Virginia. So, they said this is the time to use this urban renewal money to get these people out of here. That was the way they were thinking back then. Because if they had a plan, it would have been developed by now. So, to me, that plan wasn't planned too well either, because the greater portion of the land is still sitting there undeveloped. And they're trying to figure out a way to get a convention center in there.

Jackson issued that statement when much of the Hill was still vacant, empty for almost a quarter century after black businesses had been torn down. He reiterates what is for him a lingering complaint.

And another thing they had said, and I happened to be one that was never approached, they said that after they had bought up the property and pieced it together for development, that they would give the property owners first right on buying back. And, of course, I never heard anything where they offered anybody any of the land back. I know I wasn't approached.

Perhaps someone working for the city misled Jackson and others into believing that they would get a chance to reestablish themselves. Such a ploy would have been useful in getting cooperation from as many of the black businesses as possible. Yet the *Daily Progress* reported in 1960, during the early stages of the renewal plan, that a housing authority lawyer had said "no special provision could be made to relocate Negro businesses in the redevelopment area."[6] If that was so, what about other locations in the city? And why not in the redevelopment area? It all comes back down to the resounding question of who was urban renewal, placed as it was on the drawing boards of the late 1950s, really designed to help most.

Walter Jones is also critical of the manner in which renewal was carried out.

I don't feel that the business people on Vinegar Hill had a fair shot at their business, as far as keeping their business was concerned, because they could have had money put into it—business—and improved it, and then could have been more successful. Some were willing to sell, and some were not. And some fought it in the courts for more money, and then some of them had to go anyway.

Some kind of governmental support to salvage minority businesses would not have been a bad idea. Lacking such aid though, some former businessmen tried to accomplish the task on their own. Edward Jackson elaborates:

We tried to set up something similar to the Metropolitan Business League, to assist people in getting monies and helping them with their management problems and what have you. But, of course, we never could really get off the ground. The town was too small.

It seems the odds were against the businesses in so many ways. In addition to renewal, the demographics of the Hill had been changing. Ruth Coles explains:

Of course, some of the things in that area had changed because when the old folks died, the young ones went out and were not interested in the long run, keeping them. The area was not the same. Many of them—those that I knew as a child—were gone, because of what I said. The old folk were gone. And then, of course, by the time they got around to this urban renewal, segregation had gone. And that made a difference, like for instance the black restaurants. You know, that has been the case in many places besides Vinegar Hill.

Frank Henry even goes so far as to say that segregation was better.

I don't know whether integration helped any or made it worse. For the black race, I believe it was worse, for the black businessman, for black businesses.

And therein lies a great paradox, for who would argue against integration? We have talked about the struggle undertaken by black Charlottesville citizens to integrate public schools. How could we criticize that? Yet Henry pinpoints a dilemma. Before integration, were the black public schools that bad? Certainly they did not receive the resources allotted to white schools, and opportunities were not as great upon graduation as they were for white students. But in honestly comparing integrated public schools with the black schools just before integration, which situation was better?

Similarly, which situation was better for black businesses, particularly the small black businesses with an established clientele? Leaving aside for a moment the issue of renewal, we still are left to contemplate whether the encroaching tide of racial integration has accomplished all that it was espoused to do. Perhaps integration was inevitable, and maybe it is also the *correct* goal for us as American citizens to pursue. But how genuine indeed is the pursuit of that goal? And how do we assess the destruction of a community and loss of livelihood as part of integration's price?

Edward Jackson specifies other concerns that, combined with renewal, made restarting a business an extremely difficult proposition.

You had a rough time getting money back in those days. You know, right after the hard times back in the '30s, '29 and '30. Then after the War years—when things got better, you know, around that time—they could get a little money. But banking has been like, and still is the same way, that if you don't have collateral, you just can't get money. Almost have to have the amount of money you want, to borrow now. You almost have to have it in the bank to get it. It is a game they play with you. You know the old saying, "The rich get richer, and the poor get poorer." That will always exist. I don't care whether you're black or white. If you're poor, you're sort of in bad shape.

We had these businesses. And once you are disrupted, you hardly ever get that business started up again. And it hasn't been any great effort by anybody that I know to replace any of those businesses that were moved. A couple of them tried to relocate, and there, they didn't have as good a location in relocating as they had. They didn't have the traffic pattern or anything else. So, they ended up folding.

Then, age has something to do with it too. Age and the money. Like at my age today, if I were disrupted, it's not likely that I'm going to push too hard to get back in the business and go into a lot of debt. And the high interest rates, what have you, you know. I'm still hanging in there with it. I don't know for how much longer. It drives you up a wall.

We haven't too many minorities at this time that's been too successful in the contracting business. They tell you you can go and rent equipment, and, you know, it's very difficult to rent it at a price you're going to make something off it after you rent them. So, it's a lot of obstacles that—I don't know what kind of help we're going to need to get this done. Going to need a good grandfather to really come and grab you by the hand and lead you on, to get you into these paying fields. If you haven't had the experience and the exposure, it's pretty hard.

It is never easy starting a business. So much groundwork has to be laid, particularly in the area of financing. Jackson, though, specifies the post–World War II years as a time when even financing was easier, easier for black businesses to get started and easier for them to expand. When urban renewal caused the black businesses to be uprooted, that particular financial advantage was lost. Main Street, of course, was the city's major thoroughfare. So, when black businesses were forced to move, they also lost the advantage of constant human traffic. Furthermore, many of those businessmen were getting old, and children, if they had any, were becoming less inclined to assume responsibility for the family enterprise. The small black business was not as attractive to black children in the 1960s as it had been in prior generations. And it was not as attractive to the local banks who must have been wondering, in the wake of renewal and the approaching era of business conglomerates, what would be the point of supporting a small black business venture.

McGinness tells of the lengthy process that her husband undertook first to open his tailor shop near the University of Virginia and then, when that building was torn down, to move into Vinegar Hill.

He had the shop about twenty-some years, because his first shop was up the university. Then when they tore down a lot of old buildings, he moved from up there, down there on Vinegar Hill.

But how often can a person adjust to changing times and the plans put into motion by others? When renewal took place on the Hill, it effectively broke his spirit. Pointing to a particular section of her house, Mrs. McGinness confides that

He built down here. There's a section on the back of my house where he built. And he just built a repair shop. He built a room there. And he did repair work there until he died. He was very bitter as were most of the other people. They had no place else to go.

A situation similar to what happened with urban renewal on Vinegar Hill occurred in Toledo, Ohio, during the 1970s. Located just a few blocks from the downtown area, a flourishing Dorr Street was the predominant location for black enterprise. As in the case of the Hill, there once existed in that black Dorr Street community a doctor's office, a dentist's office, restaurants, specialty shops, and night clubs that catered to a specifically African American clientele. Interestingly enough, segregation even that late in Toledo's history actually fostered the proliferation of such businesses. There are, in fact, many who will argue that Toledo, in the 1990s (with its population of more than 300,000) has much in common with some small southern towns as they existed in the 1950s. Blacks in Toledo have very little political power, there has never been a black mayor, and the concerns of black citizens are often overlooked in the process of governmental functioning.

So, it is not particularly surprising that Dorr Street would become the target for a very special type of urban renewal. As the *Blade*, Toledo's major newspaper, reported in a 1996 article about the affair, "At first, the meetings were secret. City officials began talking about change."[7] For a $25 million project, the federal government would kick in a substantial amount, and Toledo local officials could evidently not help but perceive the whole thing as a wonderful opportunity. But the question remains (as it does in the case of Vinegar Hill): A wonderful opportunity for whom?

As was the case with Vinegar Hill, increase in urban blight in general and a rise in the crime rate in particular were most often cited by city officials as the reasons why there was a need for renewal on Dorr Street. Yet Robert Culp, president of the Toledo branch of the NAACP at the time, vehemently opposed the use of the term "urban renewal" to characterize what occurred in that midwestern city. Culp has insisted instead that what occurred on Dorr Street "was urban removal. As far as I'm concerned, it was a conspiracy. No one had any choice. They had to go."[8] Urban *removal*. A government *conspiracy*. Those are harsh words being used by a reverend to describe government action that presumably was intended to benefit the general public, in this instance the black community. And yet those very same words reflect how some of the former residents of Vinegar Hill perceive the urban renewal that took place in their neighborhood. And just as had been the case on the Hill, the loss of black enterprise on Dorr Street was a tragedy of such vast proportion that it goes beyond what can be calculated in terms of just dollars and cents. Larry Sykes, who frequented Dorr Street when it was the center of Toledo black enterprise, explains: "It was a place where you could walk down the street, and for blocks, you would see black-owned businesses.... How many places do you know where you have that today in Toledo? Look around the city. There are none."[9]

As with Vinegar Hill, we are, in the case of Toledo, inclined to ponder once again the chain of events that led to this result. Secret meetings held by a predominantly white group of government officials and businessmen. The black community informed of the plan only after it had essentially already

Top: Ironic sign, erected on Vinegar Hill after renewal, steering tourists away from the Hill toward an historic district consisting of a courthouse, old buildings, and statues that reflect a distinctly Eurocentric culture. *Bottom:* A major intersection created by urban renewal on Vinegar Hill.

been devised. Relocation of black citizens, destruction of black businesses, no chance to recapture the essence of life as it was.

Such was the tragedy of Dorr Street as well as Vinegar Hill. Yet in contemplating how renewal occurred in that latter community, Drusilla Hutchinson assumes an even broader perspective, questioning not just the extent to which renewal was implemented in Charlottesville but questioning the purported benefits of what some have summarily called "progress":

Charlottesville don't look nothing like it used to. And I told somebody that. They said, "Why, it's so much more beautiful now." I said, "Uh-uh." I said, "I liked the old Charlottesville like it was," because you felt more at ease. You could pull your car up to the store door, and you could get out and go in. And now you got to walk up the street, up the bank, to get to it. No, I don't think Charlottesville is as beautiful as then.

I'm just going to say it right plain. People is got so they want everything to shine like new money, when God didn't—He's accumulating this world and people in it, and they are forced to have what they can afford. So, why do people that have money try to make them that don't have it move out and live in places that they can't afford, just to get what little money they do have when they know they can't—Some of them can't live on it. Because they used to have enough to live off, pay their debts and everything.

Hutchinson speaks with great pride about a time when the world was much simpler, a time before the arrival of shopping malls, when the University of Virginia was nothing more than another state school. What did the changes bring for the majority of blacks who were born and raised in the increasingly prominent college town whose rents would soon grow to be among the highest in the entire United States? Rebecca McGinness further laments that

Times have changed. To a certain extent, they have a better housing condition. But the social condition is another matter. Those people lived down in there, you didn't have all this feuding and breaking in and all. People stayed at home. Children were taught to come home. The church was the social center of the black people.

I've seen a whole lot of changes in my lifetime. All of those places! They supplied people with work. Sometimes, progress is befuddling to people. Parking places where houses used to be! It's certainly so. They're leaving nothing left for the people who live in the central city. They have more hindsight than they have foresight. You know, some parts of this thing is like a dream to me.

Hindsight, as the saying goes, is 20/20. It is easy now to speculate how the urban renewal plan might have been implemented in other ways so that the interests of blacks could indeed have been better served. But McGinness also returns us to the subject of progress, a progress that disrupts lives as a matter of course on its way to some vague destination. So, the story of Vinegar Hill might perhaps be best viewed as the climb up some querulous ladder of success, another chapter, however questionable, in the history of humankind.

CONCLUSION

It is rather interesting that none of the respondents for this study mention there ever having been a law office on Vinegar Hill. Of course, lawyers came in, from outside of Charlottesville, to lead in the battle for school integration. But why were no lawyers available to represent blacks during the Vinegar Hill renewal project? It is apropos to consider whether or not a good lawyer could have employed a series of effective strategies — postponements, injunctions, or other "stays of execution." Indeed, proper legal representation might have allowed the black residents to fare better during what would become a quite serious community disruption.

Paradoxically, in the late 1950s during the early planning stages of the Vinegar Hill project, there was a young black man attending the University of Virginia. John Merchant would become the first black person in the law school's history to graduate. His father was a gardener and his mother was a domestic, so in a sense his family was a microcosm of all that the Hill held out for blacks in terms of their history and their glorious dreams of what the future in America might bring.

Law schools today have all sorts of community-based programs, most of them designed to provide students with skills that can only be obtained through hands-on interaction with situations that occur out in the real world. But such programs are only as good as the faculty who are willing to support them. There is no evidence that the Virginia law faculty was interested in supporting the blacks on the Hill. In fact, years after his graduation, Merchant conveyed, "I don't think a significant number of the faculty were thrilled with my presence."[1] Barred from attending many of his own school's events, Merchant had his hands full trying to overcome his own problems.

But now Merchant's daughter has gone on to graduate from the University of Virginia's law school. We make this point because as generations pass, we, like the sociologist William Julius Wilson, are inclined to wonder who now are "the truly disadvantaged." On one hand, Wilson argues that "long periods

111

of racial oppression can result in a system of inequality that may persist for indefinite periods of time even after racial barriers are removed."[2] And certainly, racism does not end just because antidiscriminatory laws are enacted.

Yet what should we make of Merchant's daughter and the children of certain Charlottesville blacks who have gone on to attend the University of Virginia, the same institution that had barred their own parents from full participation in the life of the school and the life of the Charlottesville community in general? Or put another way, can the advantaged great-grandchildren of Charlottesville slaves now claim that they are truly free? Wilson contends that "minority members from the most advantaged families ... reap disproportionate benefits from policies of affirmative action based solely on their group membership."[3] That sounds like a contradiction to what he had said before concerning the persistence of racial oppression even after racial barriers are removed. It sounds like a contradiction, but it is not. It is an effort to address the reality of a problem in our society that has become so mind-boggling that it would be an understatement just to say that it is complex.

There have always been blacks, even in the South during slavery, who achieved high levels of socioeconomic independence. (Sad to say, some of them were even slaveholders.) From shortly after slavery until the time of legal integration, there were blacks, including blacks on Vinegar Hill, who were wise and industrious enough to overcome the barriers, survive, and even prosper in spite of the times in which they were living. And they passed on that legacy to their children. Even when governmental programs were designed to help underprivileged minorities, those programs were often used by the children of already prominent blacks as just another mechanism to be exploited in the American way of taking advantage of any opportunity you can find.

But what of those less fortunate, that overwhelming mass of blacks who are the descendants of slaves, still caught in that institution's psychological grip, and who for one reason or another are in no position to exploit the opportunities that are ostensibly being created for their benefit? These are the children in Charlottesville who do not finish high school because their parents did not finish because the parents' parents did not have a high school. These are the children who never see a black lawyer or black doctor or black businessman because the few who exist do not frequent such places as the Westhaven Housing Project.

The Reverend Elisha Hall spoke of how the children of Westhaven are stigmatized. Teachers, counselors, and even other blacks hold out little hope for their futures. But whether it be Westhaven, Prospect, or Garrett Square (all government-sponsored housing projects in Charlottesville), it must be acknowledged that the great masses of blacks are languishing under such types of deplorable conditions, and it is our responsibility (that is, we who form the ranks of the more fortunate) to help in the effort to effect what will be a permanently legitimate solution.

In its April 1997 issue, *Reader's Digest* ranked Charlottesville seventh in the country among best places to raise a family. That result was obtained through a public opinion poll of 1,000 parents who were primarily concerned about factors such as good public schools, low crime rate, access to colleges, and affordable cost of living. One wishes that a racial breakdown of those parents was available, especially as it is observed how places like Provo, Utah; Burlington, Vermont; and Bangor, Maine, are listed in that poll among the top 20 best places to live. We would be remiss if we did not note that each of those three places has an unusually small number of blacks in its general population.

Ann Arbor, Michigan, ranked fifteenth in that poll, saw itself actually decline in terms of likableness from the number five position it had held in a different poll conducted the previous year. Still, its position in the top 20 is an enviable one, that is, until further analysis reveals a paradox that smacks of a latter-day segregation, for directly adjacent to Ann Arbor is the city of Ypsilanti, also known as "Little Detroit," where a relatively large number of blacks reside, the crime rate is high, and the school system has no stellar reputation. Even in Ann Arbor itself, success as between the black and white races is disparate. In 1996 the *Ann Arbor News* presented the frustrating information that "African-American students lagged from 20 to 50 percentage points behind their classmates in earning proficient ratings in math, science, reading and writing tests."[4] Thereby we witness a tragic discrepancy: Good public schools but a vastly disproportionate number of the black students are not doing well academically. Top-20 city, but a large number of blacks without equal access to what the polls declare makes the city wonderful.

In praising Charlottesville, the editors of *Reader's Digest* offered the following anecdote:

> It's an old joke at the University of Virginia: two undergrads pass a statue
> and one reads the inscription: "Thomas Jefferson, 1743–1826."
> "Oh," says the other, "I didn't know he was dead."[5]

That anecdote was a quite appropriate one to present because it epitomizes the extent to which Thomas Jefferson pervades so much of Charlottesville public life. Buildings and businesses are named after him, and the university that he founded evokes his image constantly as it tirelessly quotes him as its primary source of infinite wisdom.

The essential problem, however, with proclaiming Jefferson as an American hero is when one fails to acknowledge the hypocrisy that his life and indeed his legacy represent. Even as he substantially composed the Declaration of Independence, proclaiming "that all men are created equal, that they are endowed by their Creator with certain unalienable Rights ... Life, Liberty and the pursuit of Happiness," he declared blacks to be intellectually inferior, unfit to coexist in society with whites, and capable of very little beyond a life of bondage. His life of leisure, politics, creativity, and travel was largely made possible by the hundreds of slaves whose lives he exploited to sustain his luxurious style of living. The hypocrisy is further compounded by the likelihood that though he may not have regarded blacks as equal to whites, he did not mind procreating with one (Sally Hemings) and leaving in question the real identities of quite a few people whom society labels far too easily as simply African Americans.

That phenomenon is not unique to Charlottesville. And so, as we evaluate polls such as those conducted by *Reader's Digest*, we must ask to what extent the remnants of slavery remain. In presenting Kenosha, Wisconsin, as the second-best place to live in America, the article gave the example of a white family who moved into a neighborhood and had a black man as its first visitor, welcoming them to the city. He offered them the use of his lawn mower and subsequently became a friend of the family and has remained so for over a decade. The editors of that magazine were concerned to portray the "best" cities as ones that were attractive not only in the economic sense but also in terms of the prospects for racial harmony, particularly as pertains to blacks and whites.

Human interest stories of the sort that occurred in Kenosha actually occur all over the United States. But it is apropos to ask just how universal that situation is. Are blacks and whites more prone to view one another as trusted friends and neighbors or do we, as the author Toni Morrison has asserted is the case with herself, always hold part of ourselves back away from that other race with which we have so long been in opposition?

It is interesting to note that of the cities that *Reader's Digest* calls the best places to live — including Charlottesville — one could just as easily say that they are places where blacks are either repressed, separate, or virtually nonexistent. Somehow this all factors into what makes a city a great place to live. Although there are some black Charlottesvillians who attend the University of Virginia, the overwhelming majority are known simply as "the townies," never encouraged to be anything more than what the generations of black Charlottesvillians before them had been. They eke out a living in their menial occupations, listening to exceptions being referred to as the rule, waiting on the promise of America.

APPENDICES

Appendix A

Black Charlottesville residents who were interviewed for this project (most of whom lived and/or worked on Vinegar Hill before urban renewal took place there in the early 1960s):

Cora Anderson	William Jackson
Raymond Bell	Charles Johnson
Hattie Bivens	Thomas Johnson
Connie Brooks	Alies Jones
Benjamin Bunn	Walter Jones
Ruth Coles	Lionel Key
George Ferguson	Rebecca McGinness
Enola Ford	Sadie Mason
Laura Franklin	Teresa Price
Elisha Hall	Booker Reaves
Frank Henry	Alexander Scott
Drusilla Hutchinson	Commora Snowden
Thomas Inge	Mattie Thompkins
Edward Jackson	Sherman White

Appendix B

The following are questions that were used in conducting interviews. This standard set of questions was used in all of the interviews. However, it was sometimes more appropriate to allow the interviewee to deviate from the formal questioning process and elaborate in ways that our preparation of the questions could not have anticipated.

1. How long did you live in the Vinegar Hill neighborhood?
   - Were you born there?
   - Who else lived in your household while you lived there?
   - Did you own your own home? If not, who owned it?
   - Do you own your own home now?
   - How many rooms were in your house on Vinegar Hill?
   - How many rooms do you have now?
   - Who else lives in your household now?

2. Did any of your relatives (outside your household) also live on Vinegar Hill? (If yes, ask questions below)
   - How often did you see or visit each other?
   - Did you help each other in any ways? (financially, babysitting, shopping, rides to work, etc.)
   - Where did your relatives move when the area was cleared?
   - Did you see them as often after you moved?
   - Were you able to help each other as much after you moved as before?

3. Did you or others have any official or unofficial role in the revitalization plan?

4. Where did you move or to where were you moved?

5. Did you prefer the place to where you were moved as opposed to staying in Vinegar Hill?
   - Why or why not?

6. Do you feel that you and others were compensated adequately for your property and the move?

7. Was it more convenient before or after the move? (i.e. to stores, schools, friends)

8. How far back can you trace relatives who lived in Charlottesville?
   - From where did they come?
   - How long did they stay in Charlottesville? Vinegar Hill?

9. Have you ever lived anywhere else since being in Charlottesville?
   - Where?
   - How long were you there? For what purpose?

10. Within what area of Vinegar Hill did you live?
    - What was the nature of that street and area? (Ask for street name and number also)
    - What were the sanitary conditions?
    - Were neighbors more cohesive (friendlier) before or after the move?

11. What was your occupation while a resident of Vinegar Hill? Your spouse's? (What were your parents' occupations?)

• What were the various kinds of jobs held by other black people who lived on the Hill?

12. Did you and others enjoy those occupations?
    • Why or why not?

13. Was the income from your (or your parents') occupations adequate to provide for living necessities? (Before and after living on Vinegar Hill)

14. What were the other black neighborhoods that existed during the time that you lived on the Hill?
    • Were they similar to Vinegar Hill?
    • What were some differences?
    • Was the Hill itself divided into sections?

15. What schools did both you and your parents (and children) attend? Were they adequate?
    • Did school desegregation occur before or after the move?
    • In either case, what was the black reception and the overall Charlottesville reception to it like?
    • How did the move affect educational opportunities?

16. How was leisure time spent? Yours? The general Vinegar Hill population?

17. Were there any community organizations? (before and after the move)
    • What were they? Describe.

18. What church did you attend?
    • Was it located on the Hill?
    • If so, was it destroyed during the revitalization process?
    • What church do you attend now?

19. How long had Vinegar Hill been in existence before its destruction?
    • Why was it called Vinegar Hill? (Where did that name come from?)

20. Where did you and/or your parents shop when you lived on the Hill?
    • Were there very many black establishments providing goods and services for the area? (Ask for names of stores and owners)
    • Did you patronize any of them?
    • Were there any white establishments providing goods and services for the area?
    • Did you patronize them?

21. What stands out as being the most significant event that ever occurred on Vinegar Hill?

22. Were the blacks who lived on Vinegar Hill a close-knit group?
    • Describe.

- Were there sections within the Vinegar Hill area that were close-knit within themselves? Explain.
- How was group community affected by the move?
- How were you affected by the move?

23. Was there much black advancement along the socioeconomic scale during your (the) existence on (of) Vinegar Hill?
    - After the move?

24. What leaders — black or white, inside or outside of the community — do you feel have done the most for blacks?

25. Considering all that you know now, was the decision to revitalize the Vinegar Hill area, in the way that it was done, a good one or bad?
    - How did you feel about having to move then?
    - How did others feel? (Be specific if possible)
    - What was the general feeling?

Appendix C

CHARLOTTESVILLE ORAL HISTORY PROJECT
Consent Form

The Charlottesville Oral History Project is one in which selected students from the University of Virginia are working in conjunction with the Retired Senior Volunteer Program of Charlottesville to obtain information pertaining to the once prolific black community of Vinegar Hill. Materials borrowed and information obtained from interviews will be used for:

— The completion of student projects for the University of Virginia course Interdisciplinary Studies (INST) 393 — The Charlottesville Oral History Project.

— Several public presentations in the Charlottesville area (i.e. at the Bicentennial Center, churches, local libraries) to be sponsored jointly by RSVP and the University students associated with the project.

— The subject matter for approximately five radio (WINA) discussion panels that will be designed to introduce, to the public, a few of those who have worked with the project as well as the nature of the project itself.

— Written publications to be completed by Project Director James Saunders in an effort to recreate, to whatever extent is possible, life as it existed both in the area of Vinegar Hill as well as nearby Charlottesville communities.

(Once the project is completed, tapes will be preserved in an archive or manuscript collection.)

I hereby acknowledge that I have read and do understand the foregoing information; and in consideration of the work being done by the Charlottesville Oral History Project to collect and preserve, by spoken word, the culture and tradition of the particular area involved, I would like to contribute my knowledge of that community as it existed both before and after its dispersion.

_____   _____
(interviewee)   (witness)
                                                          (if the interviewee is illiterate)

_____
(date of interview)

(Optional) I do not wish to be identified as a source of information.

_____   _____
(interviewee)   (witness)

I hereby acknowledge that I have explained to _____ (interviewee) the nature of this project and how any information obtained will be used.

                                                          _____
                                                          (interviewer)

Appendix D

Diagram showing standard and substandard housing on Vinegar Hill before renewal.

NOTES

1—The Prime of Vinegar Hill

1. Helen Camp de Corse, "Charlottesville: A Study of Negro Life and Personality" (master's thesis, University of Virginia, 1933), 12.

2. Leonard Broom and Norval D. Glenn, *Transformation of the Negro American*, 2d ed. (New York: Harper, 1967), 137–38.

3. August Meier and Elliott Rudwick, *From Plantation to Ghetto*, 2d ed. (New York: Hill, 1970), 98.

4. August Meier, *Negro Thought in America: 1880–1915*, 7th ed. (Ann Arbor: University of Michigan Press, 1973), 87.

5. Elliot Liebow, *Tally's Corner* (Boston: Little, Brown, 1967), 53–54.

6. J. Wallace Jackson, "The Afro-American Experience," in *The Minority Report*, edited by Anthony Gary Dworkin and Rosalind J. Dworkin (New York: Holt, 1976), 148.

7. Meier, *Negro Thought in America*, 139.

2—Advantages and Disadvantages of Urban Renewal

1. "Redevelopment Plan for Vinegar Hill Redevelopment Project (As Amended August, 1966)," Charlottesville Redevelopment and Housing Authority.

2. "Businessmen Endorse Vinegar Hill Project," *Daily Progress*, 28 Jan. 1960, sec. 2, p. 21, col. 6.

3. "Wages, Not Housing, Cited As Local Negro Problem," *Daily Progress*, 25 Mar. 1960, sec. 2, p. 13, col. 6.

4. Ibid.

5. Ibid.

6. Charles E. Silberman, *Crisis in Black and White* (New York: Vintage, 1964), 242.

7. "Pros and Cons: Urban Renewal," *Daily Progress*, 11 June 1960, sec. 1, p. 9, col. 4.

8. "Mayor Michie Urges Voters to Support Redevelopment," *Daily Progress*, 10 June 1960, sec. 2, p. 15, col. 1.

9. Personal interview with Gene Arrington, director of the Charlottesville Redevelopment and Housing Authority, 21 October 1980.

10. Andrew Billingsley, *Black Families in White America* (Englewood Cliffs, N. J.: Prentice-Hall, 1968), 185.

11. Bernard J. Frieden, *The Future of Old Neighborhoods* (Cambridge: Massachusetts Institute of Technology Press, 1964), 25.

3—Historical Backgrounds

1. Thomas F. Johnson, James R. Morris, and Joseph G. Butts, *Renewing America's Cities* (Washington, D.C.: Graphic, 1962), 81.

2. "Referendum Information Discussed," *Daily Progress*, 30 Apr. 1960, sec. 2, p. 9, col. 7.

3. "Haggerty and Mount Urge Support of Redevelopment," *Daily Progress*, 13 June 1960, sec. 2, p. 17, col. 5.

4. 163 U.S. 537, 16 S.Ct. 1138, 41 L.Ed. 256 (1896).

5. 347 U.S. 483, 74 S.Ct. 686, 98 L.Ed. 873 (1954).

6. "Virginia," *Encyclopedia Britannica*, 1971 ed.

7. "Negro Can Be Elected Here, Former Candidate Declares," *Daily Progress*, 24 Feb. 1962, sec. 3, p. 9, col. 1.

8. "City No Longer 'Country Town,' Thompson Tells Businessmen," *Daily Progress*, 23 Feb. 1962, sec. 3, p. 13, col. 5.

9. Ibid.

10. "Forbes Urges Rejection of Vinegar Hill Program," *Daily Progress*, 13 June 1960, sec. 2, p. 17, col. 6.

11. "Close Vote Clears Way for Program," *Daily Progress*, 15 June 1960, sec. 1, p. 1, col. 8.

12. Ibid.

13. Peter Marcuse, "Abandonment, Gentrification, and Displacement: The Linkages in New York City," in *Gentrification of the City*, edited by Neil Smith and Peter Williams (Winchester, Mass.: Allen and Unwin, Inc., 1986), 154–55.

4—Relocation

1. 348 U.S. 26, 75 S.Ct. 98, 99 L.Ed. 27 (1954).

2. Ibid.

3. Personal interview with Gene Arrington, 21 October 1980.

4. Ibid.

5. Ibid.

6. Wilton S. Sogg and Warren Wertheimer, "Legal and Governmental Issues in Urban Renewal," in *Urban Renewal: The Record and the Controversy*, edited by James Q. Wilson (Cambridge: Massachusetts Institute of Technology Press, 1966), 158–59.

7. Chester Hartman, "The Housing of Relocated Families," in *Urban Renewal: The Record and the Controversy*, 321.

8. Derrick A. Bell, *Race, Racism and American Law*, 2d ed. (Boston: Little, Brown, 1973), 321.

9. Andrew Billingsley and Jeanne M. Giovannoni, *Children of the Storm* (New York: Harcourt, 1972), 87.

10. E. Franklin Frazier, *The Negro Church in America*, 8th ed. (New York: Schocken, 1972), 34.

11. John Hope Franklin, *From Slavery to Freedom*, 4th ed. (New York: Knopf, 1974), 174–75.

12. Ibid., 298.

13. Robert C. Weaver, "New Directions in Urban Renewal," in *Urban Renewal: The Record and the Controversy*, 668–69.

14. Jeanne R. Lowe, *Cities in a Race with Time* (New York: Random, 1967), 207–8.

15. Ibid., 208.

16. Jon Teaford, *The Rough Road to Renaissance: Urban Revitalization in America, 1940–1985* (Baltimore: Johns Hopkins University Press, 1990), 117.

5 — The Impacts of Urban Renewal

1. W. E. B. Du Bois, "The Souls of Black Folk," in *Three Negro Classics*, introduction by John Hope Franklin (New York: Avon, 1965), 246.

2. Jay Mandle, *The Roots of Black Poverty: The Southern Plantation Economy after the Civil War* (Durham: Duke University Press, 1978), 108–9.

3. Ray Marshall, "The Old South and the New," in *Employment of Blacks in the South: A Perspective on the 1960's*, edited by Ray Marshall and Virgil L. Christian, Jr. (Austin: University of Texas Press, 1978), 6.

4. Brian Berry, Sandra Parsons, and Rutherford Platt, *The Impact of Urban Renewal on Small Business* (U.S.A.: Keogh, 1968), 78–81.

5. Ibid., 189.

6. "City Council Approves Vinegar Hill Project," *Daily Progress*, 28 June 1960, sec. 1, p. 1, col. 5.

7. "It Was the Heart of Black Toledo ... Dorr Street," *Blade*, 18 Feb. 1996, sec. A, p. 11, col. 4.

8. Ibid., sec. A, p. 11, col. 6.

9. Ibid.

Conclusion

1. "This Time, He Is Welcome: U.Va.'s First Black Law School Grad Returns," *Richmond Times-Dispatch*, 22 May 1994, sec. C, p. 1, col. 5.

2. William Julius Wilson, *The Truly Disadvantaged: The Inner City, the Underclass, and Public Policy* (Chicago: University of Chicago Press, 1987), 146.

3. Ibid., 147.

4. "Proficiency Tests Show Stubborn Race Gap," *Ann Arbor News*, 27 Sept. 1996, sec. A, p. 1, col. 5.

5. "The Best Places to Raise a Family," *Reader's Digest*, April 1997: 79.

BIBLIOGRAPHY

Books

Bell, Derrick A. *Race, Racism and American Law.* 2d ed. Boston: Little, Brown, 1973.
Berry, Brian, Sandra Parsons, and Rutherford Platt. *The Impact of Urban Renewal on Small Business.* U.S.A.: Keogh, 1968.
Billingsley, Andrew. *Black Families in White America.* Englewood Cliffs, N. J.: Prentice-Hall, 1968.
Billingsley, Andrew, and Jeanne M. Giovannoni. *Children of the Storm.* New York: Harcourt, 1972.
Broom, Leonard, and Norval D. Glenn. *Transformation of the Negro American.* 2d ed. New York: Harper, 1967.
Du Bois, W. E. B. "The Souls of Black Folk." *Three Negro Classics.* Introduction by John Hope Franklin. New York: Avon, 1965.
Franklin, John Hope. *From Slavery to Freedom.* 4th ed. New York: Knopf, 1974.
Frazier, E. Franklin. *The Negro Church in America.* 8th ed. New York: Schocken, 1972.
Frieden, Bernard J. *The Future of Old Neighborhoods.* Cambridge: Massachusetts Institute of Technology Press, 1964.
Johnson, Thomas F., James R. Morris, and Joseph G. Butts. *Renewing America's Cities.* Washington, D.C.: Graphic, 1962.
Liebow, Elliot. *Tally's Corner.* Boston: Little, Brown, 1967.
Lowe, Jeanne R. *Cities in a Race with Time.* New York: Random, 1967.
Mandle, Jay. *The Roots of Black Poverty: The Southern Plantation Economy after the Civil War.* Durham: Duke University Press, 1978.
Meier, August. *Negro Thought in America: 1880–1915.* 7th ed. Ann Arbor: University of Michigan Press, 1973.
Meier, August, and Elliott Rudwick. *From Plantation to Ghetto.* 2d ed. New York: Hill & Wang, 1970.
Silberman, Charles E. *Crisis in Black and White.* New York: Vintage, 1964.
Teaford, Jon. *The Rough Road to Renaissance: Urban Revitalization in America, 1940–1985.* Baltimore: Johns Hopkins University Press, 1990.
Wilson, William Julius. *The Truly Disadvantaged: The Inner City, the Underclass, and Public Policy.* Chicago: University of Chicago Press, 1987.

Book Chapters

Hartman, Chester. "The Housing of Relocated Families." In *Urban Renewal: The Record and the Controversy*, edited by James Q. Wilson, 293–335. Cambridge: Massachusetts Institute of Technology Press, 1966.

Jackson, J. Wallace. "The Afro-American Experience." In *The Minority Report*, edited by Anthony Gary Dworkin and Rosalind J. Dworkin, 133–64. New York: Holt, 1976.

Marcuse, Peter. "Abandonment, Gentrification, and Displacement: The Linkages in New York City." In *Gentrification of the City*, edited by Neil Smith and Peter Williams, 153–77. Winchester, Mass.: Allen and Unwin, Inc., 1986.

Marshall, Ray. "The Old South and the New." In *Employment of Blacks in the South: A Perspective on the 1960's*, edited by Ray Marshall and Virgil L. Christian, Jr., 3–17. Austin: University of Texas Press, 1978.

Sogg, Wilton S., and Warren Wertheimer. "Legal and Governmental Issues in Urban Renewal." In *Urban Renewal: The Record and the Controversy*, edited by James Q. Wilson, 126–88. Cambridge: Massachusetts Institute of Technology Press, 1966.

Weaver, Robert C. "New Directions in Urban Renewal." In *Urban Renewal: The Record and the Controversy*, edited by James Q. Wilson, 663–72. Cambridge: Massachusetts Institute of Technology Press, 1966.

Newspaper Articles

"Businessmen Endorse Vinegar Hill Project." *Daily Progress*, 28 Jan. 1960, sec. 2: 21.

"Close Vote Clears Way for Program." *Daily Progress*, 15 June 1960, sec. 1: 1.

"City Council Approves Vinegar Hill Project." *Daily Progress*, 28 June 1960, sec. 1: 1.

"City No Longer 'Country Town,' Thompson Tells Businessmen." *Daily Progress* 23 Feb. 1962, sec. 3: 13.

"Forbes Urges Rejection of Vinegar Hill Program." *Daily Progress*, 13 June 1960, sec. 2: 17.

"It Was the Heart of Black Toledo ... Dorr Street." *Blade*, 18 Feb. 1996, sec. A: 1, 11.

"Mayor Michie Urges Voters to Support Redevelopment." *Daily Progress*, 10 June 1960, sec. 2: 15.

"Negro Can Be Elected Here, Former Candidate Declares." *Daily Progress*, 24 Feb. 1962, sec. 3: 9.

"Haggerty and Mount Urge Support of Redevelopment." *Daily Progress*, 13 June 1960, sec. 2: 17.

"Proficiency Tests Show Stubborn Race Gap." *Ann Arbor News*, 27 Sept. 1996, sec. A: 1.

"Pros and Cons: Urban Renewal." *Daily Progress*, 11 June 1960, sec. 1: 9.

"Referendum Information Discussed." *Daily Progress*, 30 Apr. 1960, sec. 2: 9.

"This Time, He Is Welcome: U.Va.'s First Black Law School Grad Returns." *Richmond Times-Dispatch*, 22 May 1994, sec. C: 1.

"Wages, Not Housing, Cited As Local Negro Problem." *Daily Progress*, 25 Mar. 1960, sec. 2: 13.

Magazine Article

"The Best Places to Raise a Family." *Reader's Digest*, April 1997: 74–81.

Court Cases

Berman v. Parker, 348 U.S. 26, 75 S.Ct. 98, 99 L.Ed. 27 (1954).
Brown v. Board of Education, 347 U.S. 483, 74 S.Ct. 686, 98 L.Ed. 873 (1954).
Plessy v. Ferguson, 163 U.S. 537, 16 S.Ct. 1138, 41 L.Ed. 256 (1896).

Article in Reference Book

"Virginia." *Encyclopedia Britannica*. 1971 ed.

Government Document

City of Charlottesville. Charlottesville Redevelopment and Housing Authority. "Redevelopment Plan for Vinegar Hill Redevelopment Project (As Amended August, 1966)."

Thesis

de Corse, Helen Camp. "Charlottesville: A Study of Negro Life and Personality." Master's thesis, University of Virginia, 1933.

Interview

Arrington, Gene (Director of the Charlottesville Redevelopment and Housing Authority). Personal interview. 21 October 1980.

INDEX